God's Priority:
World-mending &
Generational Testing

God's Priority: *World-mending & Generational Testing*

© Anne Hamilton 2017
Published by Armour Books
P. O. Box 492, Corinda QLD 4075, Australia
www.armourbooks.com

Cover Photo Credits: © Can Stock Photo/zven0
Interior scales-of-justice icon: © Can Stock Photo/AWesleyFloyd
Interior design and layout by Book Whispers

ISBN: 978-1-925380-07-1

National Library of Australia Cataloguing-in-Publication entry

Creator: Hamilton, Anne, 1954- author.
Title: God's priority : world-mending and generational testing / Anne Hamilton.

ISBN: 9781925380071 (paperback)

Subjects: Covenant theology.

              Spiritual life—Christianity.

Dewey Number: 231.76

All rights reserved. No part of this publication may be reproduced, stored in, or introduced into a retrieval system, or transmitted, in any form, or by any means (electronic, mechanical, photocopying, recording or otherwise) without the prior written permission of the publisher.

God's Priority:
*World-mending &
Generational Testing*

Anne Hamilton

Thank You

Adele
Dell
David
Donna
Lisa
Michael
Natalie
Negiel
Quang
Shing

Scripture quotations marked BSB are taken from The Holy Bible, Berean Study Bible, BSB, Copyright ©2016 by Bible Hub. Used by Permission. All Rights Reserved Worldwide.

Scripture quotations marked ESV are taken from the ESV® Bible (The Holy Bible, English Standard Version®), copyright © 2001 by Crossway, a publishing ministry of Good News Publishers. Used by permission. All rights reserved.

Scripture quotations marked GWT are taken from GOD'S WORD®, © 1995 God's Word to the Nations. Used by permission of Baker Publishing Group.

Scripture quotations marked HNV are taken from the Hebrew Names Version of the Bible. Public domain.

Scripture quotations marked KJV are taken from the King James Version of the Bible. Public domain.

Scripture quotations marked LEB are taken from the *Lexham English Bible*. Copyright 2012 Logos Bible Software. Lexham is a registered trademark of Logos Bible Software.

Scripture quotations marked NASB are taken from the New American Standard Bible®, Copyright © 1960, 1962, 1963, 1968, 1971, 1972, 1973, 1975, 1977, 1995 by The Lockman Foundation. Used by permission. (www.Lockman.org)

Scripture quotations marked NLT are taken from the Holy Bible, New Living Translation, copyright 1996, 2004. Used by permission of Tyndale House Publishers, Inc., Wheaton, Illinois 60189. All rights reserved.

Scripture quotations marked NIV are taken from the HOLY BIBLE, NEW INTERNATIONAL VERSION®. Copyright © 1973, 1978, 1984 Biblica. Used by permission of Zondervan. All rights reserved.

Scripture quotations marked NJB are from *The New Jerusalem Bible*, copyright © 1985 by Darton, Longman & Todd, Ltd. and Doubleday, a division of Random House, Inc. Reprinted by Permission.

Scripture quotations marked NKJV are taken from the New King James Version. Copyright © 1982 by Thomas Nelson, Inc. Used by permission. All rights reserved.

Scripture quotations marked NRS are taken from New Revised Standard Version of the Bible, copyright 1952 [2nd edition, 1971] by the Division of Christian Education of the National Council of the Churches of Christ in the United States of America. Used by permission. All rights reserved.

Scripture quotations marked RSV are taken from the Revised Standard Version of the Bible, copyright © 1946, 1952, and 1971 the Division of Christian Education of the National Council of the Churches of Christ in the United States of America. Used by permission. All rights reserved.

Scripture quotations marked TPT are taken from The Passion Translation™, copyright © 2011. Used by permission of 5 Fold Media, LLC, Syracuse NY 13039, United States of America. All rights reserved.

IN THIS SERIES

God's Poetry: *The Identity & Destiny Encoded in Your Name*

God's Panoply: *The Armour of God & the Kiss of Heaven*

God's Pageantry: *The Threshold Guardians & the Covenant Defender*

God's Pottery: *The Sea of Names & the Pierced Inheritance*

By the same author

Many-Coloured Realm

The Singing Silence

The Winging Word

The Listening Land

Gawain and the Four Daughters of God:
the testimony of mathematics in Cotton Nero A.x

Daystar: The Days are Numbered Book 1

More Precious than Pearls
The Mother's Blessing &
God's Favour Towards Women

(With Natalie Tensen)

Contents

Foreword		xi
Prologue		xiii
1	Tending Your Planet	1
2	The Stone That Became A Butterfly	15
3	The Xarama	41
4	From *Star Wars* to *The Green Knight*	57
5	The Bridegroom of Blood	79
6	A Comparison of Cousins	113
7	Judging Angels	139
Endnotes		153

Foreword

MENDING THE WORLD.

Overwhelming task. But one that awaits us on the 'other side' of the threshold.

This is the fifth book in this series. It's a book which, like its prequels, is one I've lived. There are sections I've struggled to bring to the page. God has overturned my view of Scriptural interpretation repeatedly as I've agonised over particular passages, trying to comprehend the inscrutability of His actions.

Why did Jesus make a walk to Emmaus His top priority on returning from heaven?

Why did God reward Phinehas with a covenant of peace for killing two people?

Why did God choose to exclude Moses from the Promised Land over something as trivial as his reaction to a Rock?

Why did Rebecca and Isaac think 'Deceiver' was a good name for a child?

Why did God spend so much time describing the nature and attributes of Leviathan to Job?

To me, these are not unanswerable questions. They are complex and difficult—and our present tendency to build 'line upon line, precept upon precept' obscures the vast sagas of Scripture that are best examined through geography.

Unless we focus from time to time on the geography, it's easy to overlook how much time Jesus spent on healing history through specific people who represented the wounded landscape around them.

This book is about the tests God places before us as we come into our calling. Like the other books in this series, it is kaleidoscopic in style. This compromise between the 'block approach' of Hebrew reasoning and the 'linear logic' of Greek philosophy is meant to deliberately challenge your mode of thinking. In addition, each section in this book is composed to conform to the ancient canons of numerical literary style. That is, it's written to achieve an exact wordcount.

I hope that, as you finish this book, you will think about God's discipline and testing in a new way. Instead of being something to dread, I hope you think to yourself: 'Bring it on!'

Anne Hamilton
Australia, 2017

Prologue

FICTION, UNLIKE REAL LIFE, has to be credible. Not too many coincidences, not too many improbable choices. Definitely no resolutions that 'deus ex machina' arrive out of nowhere, introducing a powerful rescuer whose existence was not even hinted at previously. The narrative seems contrived otherwise.

But, as the adage goes, truth is stranger than fiction.

In the aftermath of the Second Vatican Council, religious orders of Catholic nuns in Australia were directed to 'do something ecumenical'. Perhaps they were given detailed instructions or offered a list of suggestions. But I doubt it. In retrospect, to me at least, the nuns had been given so much latitude with such vague direction, they didn't really have a clue where to start.

My classroom teacher was a formidable old nun who also happened to be head of the parish primary school. Without a secretary to assist her by fielding phone calls, typing letters or running errands, she'd roster members of our class to various tasks.

One term I was on telephone duty. If the phone rang in Sister's office, I was to leave class and take a message—or, if it so happened the caller was important enough, I was to fetch Sister Mary Monica herself. One particular day I had specific instructions about a call she was expecting. If someone named 'Jack Stevens' rang, I was to inform her instantly.

I had no idea who Jack Stevens was, but I was soon to find out. He was an elderly man of stately bearing. A renowned organist, composer and choir-master, he was also a Methodist of the deepest dye and his family was well-known for their staunch religious views.

Sister Mary Monica, harassed and over-burdened in an under-resourced primary school, had—to judge by the huge beaming smile fixed to her face for days afterward—achieved an unimaginable coup. She had implemented a bravura plan while the hierarchy of nuns above her in the order were still floundering for ideas.

Our school was about to form a choir. *And* in a radical ecumenical step, that choir would be taught by the son of a Methodist minister.

One of the first songs we learned was *The Gypsy Rover*, still a favourite of mine.[1] My mum came up to the school one afternoon with my baby brother to collect my sister and me. As she watched the end of our choir practice, she took the opportunity to speak to my classroom teacher about our progress. But Sister, still glowing with victory, wanted to make sure there was no misunderstanding why a well-known Methodist was conducting a Catholic girls' choir. She effusively praised his talents and passed on all sorts of information about his background.

As she listened, my mum realised that she had once known our new choir master. Before she'd married my dad, she'd been engaged to one of Jack's best friends. Ivan, her ex-fiancé, had many traits in common with Jack. He too was a superb organist with ambitions to be a composer; he was also a staunch Methodist and the son of a Moderator of the Assembly.

Later that afternoon, my mum mentioned the new choirmaster and his older brother Tony to her mother. My grandmother started to ask probing questions as soon as she heard their names. Her whole demeanour softened when she learned that neither brother had married—information mum had gleaned from my class teacher. Tony, it transpired, had been my grandmother's fiancé long decades previously; she was stunned to know they'd both come down from the country and lived in adjacent suburbs.

Until this moment, she had never told my mother they had both been engaged to the organ-playing son of a prominent Methodist minister. Or that, in both cases, the relationship had broken up at the instigation of the man because of his family's reaction to religious differences.

My mum didn't tell me this story for many years. By that time, I too had accepted an offer of marriage from the organ-playing son of a prominent Methodist minister—and the relationship had fallen apart because of his family's reaction to religious differences.

In fact, my mum and I were exactly the same age—to the very day—when each of our engagements was broken off.

When my mum eventually pieced together these weird coincidences and unnervingly precise dates, the only frame of reference we had was to think of it as an exceedingly strange generational curse. I got prayer ministry on that basis. Yet it never felt as if the curse was dismantled. And that, I've finally realised, is because *curse* isn't the right descriptor.

It was a *test*.

And three generations failed it.

1

Tending Your Planet

THERE'S A TENDENCY IN THE RE-TELLING of Bible stories to plaster white hats on some individuals and label them 'heroes of the faith'. While the white hat is on, we skirt around the darker side of their characters and sometimes even seek to justify their failings. Naturally there's an equal tendency to plonk black hats on other individuals and ignore their good points.

This simplification into 'hero' and 'villain' has the unfortunate effect of blinding us to many significant messages of Scripture.

When it comes to the great patriarch Abraham, all sermons about testing invariably focus on the momentous, heart-wrenching trial of faith that he *passed*. He was willing to sacrifice his son Isaac at the Lord's behest.[2]

This is not the only time Abraham displays commendable faith—rabbinic tradition says God set him ten tests and he passed them all. That's a curious assessment because Abraham's faith is far from unalloyed.[3] It's a complex mixture of trust in God and fear of man.

I've yet to hear a sermon on the test of faith that Abraham *failed*. And he didn't just fail it once. Given a repeat opportunity to pass in almost exactly the same circumstances, he crashed a second time. A third opportunity to pass the same test was given to his son Isaac who made an even bigger mess of it.

These three occasions are so eerily similar that many scholars refuse to believe they all happened. Instead they consider that one single episode had been retold around campfires down the centuries and, in the narration, the facts gradually became confused. They don't see the tests. All they see is that, in one variation of the tale, Isaac is the protagonist while the two other reworkings have become attached, first to Abram, and then to Abraham.

What are these tests? The first occurs during a time of famine, when Abram took his household down to Egypt. On the way, he became concerned that his life would be in danger simply because his wife was so beautiful. The Egyptians, he thought, would kill him in order to take her for themselves.

So he asked Sarai to do her part in a plan to ensure his safety: their story was to be that they were brother and sister. Later on, we discover this isn't entirely untrue: Sarai was in fact Abram's half-sister. Nevertheless, Abram's intent was deceptive—he deliberately hid the fact she was also his wife.

Soon enough, Pharaoh got to hear of the beautiful foreigner and acquired her for his house. He loaded Abram with gifts and favour: slaves, sheep, cattle, donkeys and camels, silver[4] and gold. Make no mistake about it, Pharaoh piled incredible wealth on Abram. And in doing so, he showed how much he valued Sarai.

Not long after, Pharaoh somehow figured out that he'd been deceived. It's implicit that, when a plague struck his land and people, he'd gone searching for a cause. No doubt it took a while but finally he realised that he'd innocently and inadvertently been party to a great wrongdoing. He'd stolen another man's wife.

He was appalled. Not only at what he'd done, but also at Abram's deception. 'Why have you done this to me?' he asked.

The horror of the event is reflected in his words of dismissal. The last time the Hebrew word for 'Go!' was used in this way in Scripture was when God expelled Adam and Eve from Eden.

Abram sinned. And, perhaps significantly for later events, he became rich as a consequence.

Now at this time of his life, Abram had a relationship with God but not a covenant. Around a decade later, Abram cut the first of four covenants with God—a blood covenant. Some fourteen years later, he cut a name covenant—then six days[5] afterwards, both a threshold covenant and a salt covenant. God has told him, and confirmed, confirmed and confirmed again: *'I am your shield, your very great reward.'* (Genesis 15:1 NIV)

Abram's failure in Egypt sets the scene for his re-testing in Gerar. This occurred soon after cutting the fourth covenant. God unequivocally stated through those covenants that He would protect Abraham and his kin in all circumstances. Moreover He had promised to reward Abraham, so he would want for nothing.

Does Abraham trust God now—the best part of twenty-five years after the events in Egypt? Does he finally believe God's covenantal promises?

If he does, then perhaps a darker motive existed for his deception of Abimelech of Gerar. Perhaps—based on his experience with Pharaoh—he had no real incentive to declare the full truth. After all, Egypt had made him rich.

As I've prayed with others about the name covenants affecting their lives, I've noticed a spiritual dynamic involving the choice surrounding names. Parents often unwittingly pick ones that expose the primary unresolved spiritual issue troubling the family line.

This isn't a recent development: after all, what kind of parent names a child, *Deceiver*?

Yet Isaac and Rebecca did exactly this to their son Jacob.[6]

And the primary unresolved spiritual issue in the family line of Abraham, Isaac and Jacob was deception.

When Abraham went to Gerar soon after God's visit to him at Mamre, he realised Sarah was still stunningly beautiful. So, just as in Egypt, he feared his life might be in danger in Abimelech's kingdom. He asked Sarah to repeat the half-truth they'd used down by the Nile: to admit she was his sister but not his wife.

The story revisits the same touchpoints that occurred previously with Pharaoh. Abimelech takes Sarah into his harem. Soon disaster overtakes the kingdom: every woman in Gerar has become barren. Abimelech eventually figures out the cause in a rather dramatic revelation. He encounters God in a terrifying dream and is told he's dead because he's taken another man's wife for his own. Abimelech protests his innocence, negotiates his way out of the death sentence and wakes up in shock.

Like Pharaoh, he's taken aback with horror at what Abraham has done. In immense distress, he wants to know why Abraham has put so many blameless people in harm's way and caused such misery to the women of his nation.

It is at this point we learn Sarah is Abraham's half-sister and that they share the same father. It is also here we discover that God's promises to Abraham haven't really settled in his heart.

Abimelech then showered favour on Abraham to send him on his way. With—of course—a lavish gift of slaves, sheep and cattle. No camels or donkeys this time; instead a thousand pieces of silver.

After this—indicating, at least to me, not repentance but relief—Abraham prayed for Abimelech and his people. Then the women were healed of infertility.

So: twice in Abraham's life he was rewarded for sin and deception.

He was given a chance to re-do the test he failed in Egypt—the second time with a covenant defender on call.

But he failed again.

The responsibility for passing the test then apparently descended, with eerie exactitude, to Isaac.

It's hard to understand Abraham's mind as the situation in Gerar unfolded. Through this incident it's revealed that Abraham's heart doesn't fully trust God. Even though he'd experienced God's backing during the rescue of his nephew Lot from the might of four massive armies. With a band of just 318 household retainers, he'd pursued these armies to the far north and, in the process of saving Lot, achieved what five other armies had not—the defeat of the fourfold alliance.

Abraham was a man who could defend himself; he had human protectors as well as a divine protector. But somehow neither God nor his loyal retainers were enough security in Gerar.

Perhaps at the back of his mind, the prospect of renewed wealth beckoned. Or maybe riches meant little to him; after all, he passed up the chance to keep the legitimate spoils of war offered by the king of Sodom which would have made him rich.[7] It's ironic therefore he accepted the booty resulting from deception and sin.

In the next generation, deception and half-truth become outright lies. Isaac, also in Gerar, also having to contend with Abimelech,[8] says Rebecca is his sister—when she is, in fact, his cousin.

By the third generation, falsehood had become threaded into the family's identity. This is clear when Isaac and Rebecca name one of their twins, 'Deceiver'. The deliberate falsehood had also—apparently—warped the test as it passed down the line to Jacob.

Jacob's uncle Laban tricked him resoundingly. While the situation was not precisely similar—as it had been for Isaac and Abraham in their respective meetings with Abimelech—the same elements are there, now seriously mutated. The fundamentals of deception, of a desired bride and a sister substitution, of an overly large payment for a cousin, all play out in Jacob's wedding.

To ensure we, as readers, get the connection between this event and Abram's failure to be honest with Pharaoh, we even have the very same words spoken. They are there to help us see how the sins of the fathers impact on their children's children.

Jacob said to Laban on discovering he'd spent the night with Leah and not Rachel: 'What is this you have done to me?'

The last time those exact words appear in Scripture was when Pharaoh confronted Abram. On finally discerning the cause of the plague devastating Egypt, he sent for Abram and said: *'What is this you have done to* **me***?'*

His anguished question reflects the almost identical words of

Abimelech to Abraham: *'What is this you have done to **us**?'*

Words repeated precisely in a later generation when Abimelech tackled Isaac.

Words that are an ancient echo of Eden. *'What is this you have done?'* God asked Eve.

Pharaoh's dismissal of Abram also reflects the expulsion from the testing ground of Eden.

A test isn't a curse. But it can mutate into one.

'...the teacher is always quiet during the test.'

God's Not Dead 2

In every generation, we're called to pass the test our forebears have failed. To end the cycle of sin. To repair the harm, as far as possible, done to innocent people injured simply because they happened to be on the testing ground.

How many Egyptians died in the plague unleashed by Abram's deception? Prayer could not undo that. Sure, it could undo the barrenness of women of Gerar—but we have to wonder at what kind of witness Abraham was giving about God. It looks like, in keeping covenant with His chosen, God has afflicted an innocent population and handed their king a death sentence—while allowing His favoured one to be materially rewarded for *failing* a test of trust a second time.

Allowances could well be made for the people of Gerar if they wondered what kind of God tolerated such a perversion of justice and inversion of righteousness. Even though God protected them from sinning, He appeared to be enormously biased.

Of course He was!

Eventually Abimelech figured this out and asked to cut a covenant with Isaac. This brought to an end the consequences for the people of Gerar—but not for the family line of Abraham and Isaac.

You may not know what your ancestors have done. It's unlikely you have any idea what divine tests they have passed or failed. I happen to be incredibly fortunate that the choir-master at my school during my primary years was my grandmother's former fiancé's brother. Had he not been appointed, my grandmother wouldn't have had any reason to reveal a significant relationship from her past. And, a decade later, my mother wouldn't have had a flash of insight and realised that a mysterious pattern existed across three generations—mother, daughter and granddaughter—and bothered to tell me about it.

In some families, the silence covering previous generations is so intense that we may never know whether repeated patterns are in play. Yet we may have a sense there is and, when we do, there's a significant question to ask.

Is the situation a curse?

Is it a test?

A curse has already been dealt with at the cross of Jesus. We can simply pray that it be nailed there and declared dead.

A test is a different matter. We can't pray it away. We can only pray for the empowering grace to pass. All divine tests come down to the same basic question: 'Do you trust God in *this* situation?'

For Abraham, he could trust God to keep His promise about a son, however long-delayed. And he could trust God to save and preserve that son's life. He was willing to offer Isaac as a sacrifice, having faith that God would resurrect him, if necessary. (Hebrews 11:19) He could also trust God when it came to Ishmael. Despite his reluctance to acquiesce with Sarah's wishes, he banished Hagar and Ishmael—trusting that God would bring His promises for them to pass.

But did he trust God to protect him and Sarah in a foreign land? No. In *that* situation, he couldn't bring himself to rely on God totally.

In a later age, when God announces His exemplars of righteousness through the prophet Ezekiel, Abraham doesn't make the list.[9] Noah and Daniel do, along with Abraham's contemporary, Job.

In fact, in an ironic twist of timing, Abraham was in the process of failing his second test while Job was scratching his way to a pass mark in a separate, immensely more difficult test, about a hundred kilometres east.

I conclude that both these tests have to have occurred simultaneously because, while it is possible two unusual cosmic impact events could have occurred in the same area within a short interval of years, it seems far more likely that just one did.

The story of the destruction of Sodom and the cities of the plain is clearly the description of a meteoric impact as experienced at virtual ground zero. The opening of Job is equally clearly the description of a meteoric impact as experienced a short distance from ground zero. The strange wind that levels the house, killing all Job's children, fits a shockwave accompanying an impact event. The sudden descent of so many raiders on his livestock is consistent with mobs looting, even while in their flight from catastrophe. Job's skin eruptions suggest an illness resulting from a nuclear-like explosion. Moreover, Job lived in the land of Uz—which appears, from the names mentioned in connection with it, to have been on the east bank of the Jordan, not far from the site identified by archaeologist Steven Collins as the impact-blasted ruins of the city of Sodom.

Like Pharaoh and Abimelech, Job was caught on the testing ground. His innocence is never in question.

Sure, in the courts of heaven, Job was—though he didn't know it—God's appointed champion. On earth, however, Job's misfortunes were simply part of the collateral damage as Sodom was destroyed.

The ordeal he was set makes Abraham's test look like it belongs in kindergarten. As for Adam and Eve's test in Eden, theirs was ridiculously simple by comparison.

Yet, as Philip Yancey points out, Adam and Eve in the best-case scenario fail their test while Job, under the worst possible circumstances, passes his.[10]

As Jesus does—some two thousand years later.

Until the time came to fulfil his dreams, the Lord tested Joseph's character.
Psalm 105:19 NLT

Abraham's second test occurs not long after he has undertaken a threshold covenant[11] and a salt covenant with God. Directly after this dual covenant event, Abraham walks with God, as any good Bedouin host would still do, to see Him safely on the right path. During this walk, God reveals He is heading for Sodom and Gomorrah to investigate the outcry that has reached heaven about them.

Abraham begins bargaining with God regarding the judgment hanging over the five cities of the plain. As indicated in previous books in this series, this is not a coincidence. Once we have a holy threshold covenant in place with God and we have 'passed over' the Cornerstone, we are called to negotiate with Him on behalf of people and places and happenings.

'Will not the Judge of all the Earth do right?' (Genesis 18:25 NIV)

Although this question forms part of Abraham's plea on behalf of Sodom, it perfectly summarises Job's entire complaint against God.

Neither he nor his friends can work out what was going on in Job's life. They had a neatly packaged theological understanding of God that had been shredded. As Philip Yancey says: 'God's justice has collided head-on with Job's innocence. Nothing makes sense any more.'

And Job, audaciously and with—as far as his friends are

concerned—scandalous effrontery, asked for a personal explanation from God.[12] Yet behind his boldness is a remarkable attitude. Yancey points out: 'Job may have given up on God's justice but he steadfastly refuses to give up on God.'

Eventually, after Job lays out a formal legal defence of his innocence, God appears in a whirlwind. His speech to Job is variously described as 'blistering' (Philip Yancey), 'scandalous' (Gerhard von Rad), 'sneering, jeering' (George Bernard Shaw), 'highly discordant' (Peter Lockwood).

It took me a while to realise these authors were serious.

I've never seen it that way. I've seen a majestic and also magisterial set of rhetorical questions that encode wondrous, allusive answers to matters Job had previously raised. My heart has always leapt in response to God's appearance and the vast extent of the hidden knowledge He takes out of His treasury and ever-so-casually passes to Job.

What does He tell Job? The longest section of God's speech is about Leviathan. His description of the creature explains in the simple language of the natural world what the wildfire spirit of this fallen seraphim is like.

It's only once we realise that Job was caught up in the backlash of threshold covenant violation involving the city of Sodom that we can see in God's words an explanation of what has happened. Job and his family were, unfortunately and despite their innocence, collateral damage when justice was meted out over the perpetration of dishonour so rank that its stink reached to heaven itself.

Honour is like fragrant incense before the throne of God; dishonour a stench.

God is actually honouring Job with a confidence; He hasn't peremptorily dismissed him with questions designed to put him in his place, as so many commentators seem to think. Even if those questions were designed to put Job in his place—which I seriously dispute—look at what that place is. He is a man, mortal and distressed with disease, who has *summoned God into his presence*—insignificant as he is, he has called on God. And God has *answered*.

The 'Job scenario' is the most difficult of all places to be when it comes to tests. Sometimes we are caught up in trials and adversities that are generational curses; sometimes these ordeals are generational tests. But sometimes we have no responsibility for events: like Job, we're innocent bystanders who get caught up, through no fault of our own, on someone else's testing ground.

Lest we should feel sorry for ourselves as 'innocent bystanders' crushed by events beyond our control, God has appointed us to an exalted position. We are His champions. We're called to show cosmic entities like Leviathan and the satan the nature of God's wisdom. (Ephesians 3:10)

When Job, at the end of his story, is rewarded with a double portion of all he lost, he doesn't receive twice as many children as before. Just another set. Telling us that his first set was not truly lost but would be restored to him.

A test is not a punishment but part of God's spiritual training for us that helps shield us from sin. *'Do not be afraid; for God has come only to test you and to put the fear of Him upon you so that you do not sin.'* (Exodus 20:20 NRS)

A test is also part of mending the world.

'It's a question of discipline,' the little prince told me later on. *'When you've finished washing and dressing each morning, you must tend your planet.'*
Antoine de Saint-Exupéry, *The Little Prince*

Now we might think that, because Jesus was perfect, there were no tests He had to redo after He crossed that ultimate threshold: that of death into resurrection.

But that would not appear to be entirely true.

Think about what happened on the day of His resurrection.

He met Mary Magdalene in the garden early in the morning.

He met Cleopas and his companion on the way to Emmaus late in the afternoon.

He met ten of His disciples in an upper room later that evening.

Presumably most of the day was spent with His Father. After all, He said to Mary, 'Don't touch Me! I have not yet ascended to the Father.'[13]

Now His top priority on coming back from the Father was not to reassure His frightened disciples, to comfort His grieving mother or set the minds of His shocked friends in Bethany at rest. Instead it was to meet two people never previously[14] mentioned on a short journey to a small rural village about ten kilometres from Jerusalem. Isn't this all a bit odd?

Come to think of it, Jesus' behaviour during His remaining forty days on earth is exceptionally odd. We have no idea where He was or what He was doing most of the time. Or do we?

Perhaps there are hints of His agenda in the stories we do have.

For instance, in the conversation with Mary Magdalene, there are allusions to the bridal encounter in the Song of Songs. But the most obvious echo is to God's words in the Garden of Eden: *'Where are you?'*

This is the moment of Eden overturned; set right—reversed. Where the representatives of humanity come looking for God, instead of God looking for them.

Check out again Jesus meeting with ten of His disciples in an upper room. Two are missing: Judas, who has killed himself, and Thomas. When Thomas returns, he refuses to believe Jesus has appeared to the other ten. Here we have twelve men, divided into two groups—ten professing faith, two influenced by doubt. The allusion in the incident is to the time the twelve spies entered the Promised Land—returning to their hidden encampment at Kadesh Barnea, similarly divided into two groups: ten influenced by doubt, two professing faith. The name Thomas confirms the allusion.[15]

Jesus prepares for the curse of Kadesh Barnea to be reversed later that week—when the representatives of the twelve tribes all agree in faith to go forward into the future Jesus promised.

Still later, there's a personal reversal, of course. Simon Peter is given three chances by Jesus to confirm his love—reflecting the three denials in the courtyard of Caiaphas.

And then there's the coming of the Holy Spirit at Pentecost: a reversal of the curse of both of Babel—where language scattered men over the earth. It also reverses the incident involving the golden calf. At Sinai, three thousand men died. At Pentecost, three thousand men were saved.

So, let's go back now to that mysterious journey to Emmaus recorded in Luke 24:13-35. It is apparently the first thing Jesus does on returning from the Father. It has top priority after undoing the curse of Adam's sin in the Garden outside the tomb.

What on earth could have been so damaging that it tore the world apart almost as much as the sin of Adam?

There's an early tradition identifying the companion of Cleopas as his wife. John identifies that wife as Mary[16] and an aunt of Jesus.[17] So, if this were another reversal of threshold covenant violation, it would have to go back to a Scriptural event involving a man and his wife en route from one place to another—accompanied by another man.

Only two obvious scenarios fit. The first involves Moses, Zipporah and their son, Gershom, on their way to Egypt. They stop at an inn and, in one of the most inscrutable passages of Scripture, God tries to kill Moses. Zipporah's swift intervention with the covenant-sealing action of circumcision saves Moses' life. '*Surely you are a bridegroom of blood to me!*' she says. (Exodus 4:25 NIV)

Frankly I think Zipporah had much to learn about a bridegroom of blood. She might have been right about Moses, but he was seriously outclassed by his grandson Jonathan.

Jonathan, Gershom's eventual son, was the Levite who travelled with his concubine and his servant from Bethlehem, heading for the hill country of Ephraim.

This tragic journey involves one of the most gruesome episodes in Scripture, involving the rape and murder of the concubine. Her death led to the almost complete annihilation of the tribe of Benjamin. It also led to generations of feud and hatred between the people of Bethlehem and those of Gibeah, the hometown of Saul, Israel's first king. In addition, it led to the installation of an idolatrous sanctuary in northern Israel where golden calves were worshipped. This shrine in the city of Dan, near Caesarea Philippi, was serviced by Jonathan and his descendants.

And this whole vile and far-reaching episode is what I believe Jesus was reversing on the road to Emmaus. He joined a man and his wife—a man with a suitably symbolic name linking him to that shrine in Dan. Cleopas is the male counterpart of Cleopatra—a name most often connected with the queen of Egypt, who happened to have been deeded the land around Caesarea Philippi some seventy years beforehand. His name, *keys of the fatherland*,[18] echoes the words of Jesus to Simon Peter at Caesarea Philippi: '*I give to you the keys of the kingdom of heaven...*'[19]

At Emmaus we see the bridegroom of peace undoing the curse of the bridegroom of blood. In breaking the bread and commemorating His own broken body, we also find echoes of the cut-up body of the concubine, the pieces of which had been used as a call to war.

This incident at Emmaus should be incredibly reassuring for us as we face the prospect of having to redo the tests our ancestors have muffed. The reversal doesn't have to be an overwhelming, taxing, harrowing event. It can be as simple as asking someone to dinner.

That's what the story of Emmaus reveals.

Cleopas and his wife were on a testing ground. All they did was to invite Jesus to share it with them. So they are a model for us: just invite Jesus onto the testing ground with us—to help us influence the outcome of generational tests we're asked to redo.

Because, simple—almost trivial—as it seems, sometimes all we have to do to mend the world is invite someone over for a meal.

2

The Stone That Became A Butterfly

I LOVE METEORITES. SO IT SHOULD BE no surprise one of my favourite Scripture verses hides a reference to falling starstuff. It was a favourite long before I discovered its concealed layer. And when I did, I wasn't entirely surprised at my choice: the older I get, the more I understand I'm drawn towards mirrors of my own name.

'Anne' has had a mythic[20] entanglement with meteorites for millennia. Though, strictly speaking, it's more accurate to say the names from which 'Anne' is derived have those entanglements. While almost any book will tell you it's from Hebrew and means 'grace', it's far more complex than that.

In European culture, it became attached to names like Anna Perenna—originally an Etruscan mother goddess who become the Roman goddess of the returning year. It's also linked with Ana and Danu—Celtic mother goddesses. Often these divinities were triple goddesses like the Graces and Furies of ancient Greece.

The dark mothers were often first worshipped as heaven-dispensed meteorites.

Despite this affinity, I'm not quite sure how I'd seen through the English translation of Job 38:36 and discerned the falling star there—perhaps it was the mention of constellations a few verses earlier. Whatever the reason, I'd always felt deeply stirred while reading Job 38:36 NIV—*'Who endowed the heart with wisdom or gave understanding to the mind?'*[21]

The word rendered as *heart* is 'sekviy'; also meaning *meteor*. This is the sole appearance of 'sekviy' in Scripture. Although it's been traditionally translated *heart*,[22] the immediate context is clouds, lightning, ice, frost and starry clusters. So perhaps it's better translated *meteor*. Yet if it were, we'd miss its psychological and spiritual aspects.

This relationship between *heart* and *meteor* perhaps explains the seemingly abrupt transition from verse 3 to 4 in Psalm 147: *'He heals the broken-hearted and binds up their wounds. He determines the number of the stars and calls them each by name.'* (NIV)

Like other words explored in this series, *heart* and *meteor* are considered so disparate in modern culture[23] it's all but impossible to burrow inside the mindset that intimately related them within 'sekviy'.[24]

Perhaps the overarching idea was *kernel*. A meteorite is the kernel of a spacerock whose shell is burned off in its shining flight through the atmosphere. Similarly our heart is the core and kernel of our being.

Many people see God's 'sekviy' question as part of a tirade. Basically: 'Hey, man, don't question Me! You're outta line! Don't you know I'm Almighty God and can do as I please?'

I can't see it as a tantrum. Strike up a symphonic orchestra. The appearance of God in Job 38 is soul-stirring stuff. It's time for answers.

Ten chapters previously Job had asked where wisdom comes from. *'But where shall wisdom be found? Where is the place of understanding?'* (Job 28:12 HNV)

And six chapters previously Elihu had said, *'It is the spirit in man, the breath of the Almighty,*[25] *that makes him understand.'* (Job 32:8 ESV)

The word Elihu uses for *breath*, 'nashamah', is related to the word for the human *soul* and encodes the world for *name*, 'shem'. It's a highly nuanced word which suggests we receive a soul when God creates us by whispering a name to us.[26] The first time 'nashamah' appears in Scripture is when God breathes a soul into Adam:

And the Lord God formed man of the dust of the ground, and breathed into his nostrils the breath [nashamah] of life; and man became a living soul.

Genesis 2:7 HNV

In His speech, God clarifies Elihu's words about the origin of wisdom when He asks about 'sekviy'. He offers more information. The question encodes an answer.

In fact, God hides a wealth of information in His questioning. For example, the mention of the constellation of Orion just before the question about the 'sekviy' seems to suggest a radiant vector[27] for a meteor strike: *'Who* [makes]*... the waters become hard as stone, when the surface of the deep is frozen? Can you bind the chains of the Pleiades? Can you loosen Orion's belt?'* (Job 38:29-31 NIV)

In the same sequence, the reference to the sea frozen like a stone sounds like the results of an impact winter.[28]

These divine 'questions' therefore, in my mind, link back to the tragedies that overtake Job as his story starts. Fire drops out of the sky, killing his herds of sheep. A whirlwind rips up out of the desert, collapsing the house of his eldest son where his children are all feasting. Several different bands of raiders take off with his cattle, donkeys and camels.

Those details correlate incredibly closely with a cosmic impact event and its destructive aftermath: the fireballs from heaven, the shockwave and pressure wind, the refugees stealing what they can.

Until a meteor exploded over the town of Chelyabinsk in a relatively uninhabited part of Russia on 15 February 2013 causing over 1100 injuries, most people remained sublimely ignorant of the frequency of meteors entering the earth's atmosphere and the potential damage they could cause. When asked the proper response if such a bolide were to head for a more inhabited region, NASA offered some prudent advice: 'Pray.'

At the beginning of the second century before Christ, during the ascendancy of the Roman empire, a few dozen meteorites are thought to have slammed into southern Germany. Hitting the ground at the incredible speed of ten kilometres *per second*, they exploded on impact, liquefied the ground and sent melted rockshatter hurtling high into the atmosphere. The effect was like a couple of hundred atomic bombs going off simultaneously.

From afar, it would have looked as if a forest of immensely tall, white and glittering trees instantly mushroomed into existence on the horizon. From closer in, no one would have survived to describe it.

An hour or so after impact, a few hundred kilometres to the east, hot glassy leaf-shaped arrowheads would have startled people by dropping without warning out of the sky. This melted rockshatter fell back to earth, aerodynamically shaped into arrows by its sub-orbital tumble. To those experiencing the sudden attack, an unseen army of elves must have been responsible.

Today, the tranquil lakes around Tüttensee belie their probable explosive origin. Today we also know quite independently through dendrochronology that, in 207 BC, the climate of Europe underwent sudden, drastic collapse. There was no summer—crops failed when the growing season simply vanished.

The two events may be unrelated. But it seems unlikely.

Just so, the story of Job and the story of the destruction of Sodom and Gomorrah may be completely unrelated. But that also seems to me to be incredibly unlikely.

Germination includes the hatching of a meteor and the tap of a swallow's beak breaking the egg, and it guides the birth of the earthworm, and the advent of Socrates.

Victor Hugo, *Les Misérables*

As a fiction writer I often try to help others just starting out. Frequently I find aspiring writers resistant to the literary technique, 'point of view'. They assert vehemently, 'It's a fad. Why should I strain at re-working my manuscript because of a passing fashion?'

Now, I not only think 'point of view' is a very valuable technique, I don't think it's a fad. I believe it's been around since the oldest book of the Bible was written. I'm not particularly concerned if you think the oldest book is Job or Genesis.

Not only does the book of Job ask the question any believer in a good God finds most difficult to answer—why innocent people suffer—but, as I've indicated in the last section, it almost certainly preserves 'the other side' of one of Scripture's most controversial stories.

Two impact events described in the Bible occurred about the same time in the same vicinity. Now, while it's possible they are entirely separate catastrophes, it's much more likely the two eye-witness accounts relate to exactly the same incident.

Job recounts one side of the story from the perspective of a resident of Uz.

Genesis, in describing the destruction of Sodom and Gomorrah, offers an entirely different 'point of view'.

On the one hand we have the story of a young and greedy man who only just escapes the destruction of his city with his family—for no better reason than that his uncle has God as his covenant defender; and it happens that that relationship between God and his uncle includes him under its umbrella.

On the other hand, we have an innocent, just and generous man whose entire family is wiped out—despite that man's close relationship with God.

As Jesus said: *Your Father... in heaven... sends rain on the just and on the unjust.* (Matthew 5:45 ESV)

He might just as well have said *meteorites*, not *rain*.

Still there's something to notice about Abraham and Job: one has not just one—but four!—covenants with God; there is no indication the other had progressed beyond a deep, abiding relationship.

Yet it is out of their intimacy with God that each is asked to pray for others.

Abraham did the wrong thing to Abimelech; yet, despite his guilt, it was still *his* prayers that would avail for the people of Gerar.

Job's friends did the wrong thing; yet, despite Job's innocence, it was not their prayers for him that would avail but *his* for them.

Prayer is not about our relative righteousness in any situation; it is about our relationship with God.

When I was much younger I had a spiritual fantasy. Other people may have desired to be prophets or apostles, evangelists or famous teachers—but my secret desire was to experience the end of the book of Job. I wanted God to appear out of a whirlwind and ask in a majestic, thunderous voice: 'Who is this who darkens My counsel with words without knowledge?'

I had my response all planned. 'With respect, Sir, it's *me*.'

Even as a child, I'd figured out something important about the relationship between God and people. It didn't matter how many sermons people imbibed or how much theology they studied, they reacted from the beliefs hiding in their hearts. These beliefs were almost entirely immune to outside forces—like sermons, exhortations, positive thinking seminars, self-help books and theological training. Sure, a blip could occur in people's thinking but they soon returned to a default position.

My mum once had a conversation with the local minister. 'One thing I am sure of,' he said. 'There is not a single person in this congregation who doesn't have a deep assurance God loves them.'

My mum was doubtful. 'Really? How do you know that?'

'Every Sunday, for over twenty years, I've preached that truth.'

My mum went away and asked around two dozen stalwarts of the church—many of whom had been sitting under the minister's preaching for all of those twenty years—whether they really believed God loved them. Only two did.

I didn't find this a surprising result. It's easy to sense some people feel like worms before God and some like giants. Some people petition Him in grovelling tones, half-expecting no response; others simply order Him around, telling Him He's made a promise and He'd really better keep it. And there's a whole spectrum in between.

I didn't want to be either a bossy boots or a bit of used chewing gum on the bottom of God's shoe. Nor did I want to be balanced, half-way between the extremes; I sensed that was to fall into a trap of mediocrity.

Instead I wanted to be like Job—simultaneously infinitesimal and supreme. I wanted the paradox of mortified and uplifted, crushed and exalted.

My spiritual fantasy had me melting with pleasure as God gave a dramatic rendition about the wonders of the universe, about Behemoth, about Leviathan. I was sure translators had added tones of sarcasm to God's voice that weren't there. *'Where is the way to the dwelling of light...? ...You know, for you were born then, and the number of your days is great!'* (Job 38:19-21 ESV)

Take out that exclamation mark, meant to indicate scorn, and God's comment becomes a statement, a hint we already have access to this knowledge.[29]

I nourished this spiritual fantasy for years, never expecting it to really come to pass. But one day I was sitting with a coffee, talking to God, when He arrived. Not in a physical whirlwind. The best I can do to describe the sensation is to say it was an irruption. A sudden wild intrusion into the relative calm of my mind and emotions; a Voice asking: 'Who is this who darkens My counsel with words without knowledge?'

I was so stunned, I went into flustered panic. I couldn't remember what response I'd planned in my daydreams. All thought had dissipated.

'Now,' said God, 'about the answers. The first and most significant is: the heartstone of the problem is Nuada.'

'What? *Answers?!*' I found my tongue. 'No, no—this is wrong! You're supposed to ask questions...' I broke off, transfixed by a stern silence. It felt like moving out of the wall of a whirlwind into its eye.

'You,' God informed me, 'are *not* Job.'

Oh yeah, I gulped. *I am not Job. I've made a terrible mistake. I've wanted to be like Job. I should have wanted to be like me.* 'So I get answers, not questions?'

'The heartstone of the problem is Nuada.'

'What's that mean?'

There was no answer. None at all. The irruption was gone.

So I wasn't Job and so I got answers, not questions. But I was sure I needed to find the question belonging to the answer.

And I assumed God's answer would:
- be important to me personally
- be important to others as well
- contain the original question in coded form

That was the way He had presented his questions to Job. With this in mind, over the next year, I chased the words 'heartstone' and 'Nuada' through different languages, across legendary landscapes, through ancient myth, down dead ends of folklore. Nuada, it quickly transpired, was a Celtic god-king. He had lost his kingdom when, during a battle, his hand was slashed off.

I followed up almost any kind of lead—excepting those that headed in the direction of New Age teaching or the occult. I asked questions of anyone who would sit still long enough and humour my inquiries. Some people thought I was talking about a 'heart of stone': a hardening of the heart due to a habit of emotional or spiritual withdrawal. But I was reasonably confident that was not what God had meant.

About six months into the journey I was able to translate His words: 'The merlin of the problem is Merlin.' Which, while suggesting I had been going down the right path, wasn't particularly helpful.

As I became familiar with different cognate words for *heart* in Celtic, I discovered these were also the words for *mind* and *soul*. Likewise in Old Norse, the word for *heart* was also that for *mind* or *soul*.

I wondered for a while if I should be looking for 'mindstone' or 'soulstone'. Eventually I came to the conclusion that any answer simply had to encompass those possibilities as well.

Meantime, my researches uncovered the possibility that the famous ravens, Thought and Memory—Munin and Huginn—of

Teutonic mythology could just as easily be known as *Mind* and *Soul* or *Mind* and *Heart*. Each day, Munin and Huginn are said to travel the world, reporting back to Odin, the triple All-Father of northern legend, what they have spotted during their flight.

Now, spend lots of time with 'Odin' and its variant spellings or with 'Huginn' and its cognates and—sooner or later, if you investigate the root words and associated names[30] back far enough—you're bound to encounter a Jesus or two.

It comes as a shock to the majority of Christians to discover there is a 'spirit of Jesus'—a counterfeit—who works the system well. It also comes as a relief to a small minority of Christians to discover there is a counterfeit Jesus. They've encountered the false one and were troubled and baffled by its darkness. They felt unable to ask if anyone else was assailed by this savage, sacrifice-demanding deity.

It's for very good reasons that the Church, over the centuries, has adopted creeds and confessions. Today, when someone comes out of witchcraft they're likely to ask for clarification about the statement, 'Jesus is Lord.'

'Which Jesus?' is a legitimate question.

One of the Celtic words for *heart*, 'uis'—pronounced 'wis' or 'whis'—derives, according to a surmise of the great linguist and fairytale-collector, Jakob Grimm, from the same root as the name, Hesus.

This is essentially the same name as Jesus. However Hesus is a bloodthirsty Germanic god of the forests from the same time period as Jesus of Nazareth. Eventually Hesus seems to have evolved into Odin of the three hundred names.[31]

When I first came across Grimm's hypothesis during my research into *heartstone*, I'd done enough investigation of names to understand instantly the ramifications of this. Whatever the *heartstone* was, it was a place where Jesus was supposed to reign. But the heart is deceitful and wicked above all things, so if His throne had been usurped by someone who claimed His name, how would I know?

So, in shock, I immediately turned to God in prayer: 'Lord God, I have never ever deliberately prayed in the name of any god who might have usurped the name of Jesus of Nazareth, but *if* I have—*if* on any occasion ever I have unconsciously done so—then I repent and ask You to forgive me. And by the way, I pray this in the name of Jesus *of Nazareth*.'

As I finished, I saw in my mind's eye, a python rising out of my head. I cannot begin to describe my horror or my bafflement.

It took me years to realise the significance of the python in relation to the emphatic 'if' of my prayer. Python is a threshold guardian and, although I had no idea that I was making an effort to clean up my sekviy, Python was alarmed enough to flee. And God was gracious enough to permit me to see it in flight.

Sekviy: when I finally found the word and discovered it was slap-bang in the middle of one of my favourite Scripture passages,[32] it seemed like I'd been dancing with the concept, without ever recognising it, half my life. Neither a fleshly heart turned to stone, nor a stone softening into a beating heart, a sekviy is both a meteorite and the spiritual core of a human being.

I finally identified 'sekviy' as the *heartstone* God had spoken of because I'd spent a lot of time investigating the other word He'd given me: Nuada.

Sure it's the name of a Celtic god but, in the end, I'd decided Nuada originally was a comet. And meteorite showers are quite often the remains of comets. The Orionids, for example, of late October are the result of Earth passing through the orbit of a pile of stones which come from Halley's Comet.

In my view, any *heartstone* that fitted the answer God gave me had to have something to do with a comet or meteorite. I'm pretty sure I know what you're thinking. I've been there. I've thought that it's totally crazy to even consider a *meteorite* could possibly be the same as the *spiritual core of a human being*. How could our foundations be like falling stars? How can a soul be the same as a rock from space? Even a rock as beautiful as an iron meteorite with its fine interleaved crystals and the stunning geometrics of its Widmanstätten patterns?

The Greeks, with their use of 'psyche',[33] convinced us that a soul is as fragile and ephemeral as a butterfly. That's what psyche means: both *soul* and *butterfly*.

But what if a soul is as adamantine as diamond, as sharp as fire-hardened iron, as radiant as a comet?

What if we really are, just as the Hebrews thought, woven stone?

Living stones: metaphor or reality?

We are composed of the same chemicals as clay, after all, which when deposited and put under pressure turns to sedimentary rock.

The word 'sekviy', *heartstone*, is explicit in Job but implicit in Genesis.

When God and Abraham covenanted with bread and salt at the threshold, they were together at Abraham's tent. God was actually on His way to Sodom with two angels when He stopped by. During this visit, they undertook the union of a third and then a fourth covenant—the first of these pacts, the blood covenant, had been cut fourteen years previously and the second, the name covenant, a mere six days beforehand.

Now this threshold covenant includes a very specific promise. It was along very much the same lines as previous promises God had offered Abraham in the past. However it now included a precise time for the fulfilment of the promise: *within a year you will be the father of a son to be called Isaac.*

Flash of light, quickening of a womb: when God breathed the name 'Isaac', a soul was created.

As we saw back at the beginning of this chapter, it is when God whispers a name that the way is prepared for conception.

Normally a threshold covenant is solemnised as the guest passes over the cornerstone of a house to be welcomed by the host. It's more than probable that God spoke these words, '...*in a year you will be the father of a son to be called Isaac,*' right at the moment He crossed the threshold stone into Abraham's tent. After all, He uses a threshold word: 'Isaac'.

The name Isaac—Yitshaq—does indeed mean *he laughs*, as is usually recorded in lexicons; but hidden in it is the word for *lintel*.[34]

And there is a deep significance to passing over the stone in God's action: the special word for the basin-shaped threshold stone used to catch the sacrificial blood painted on the lintel and doorposts is 'kaph'.[35] However the general word for *stone* in Hebrew is "eben'.

This is the first threshold covenant between God and His chosen people alluded to in Scripture. So it's the threshold of thresholds as it were.[36]

God Himself is the creator of the stone—and He speaks over it the words of His promise. He sanctifies the threshold stone as He crosses over it, declaring words about *father* and *son*, here in this *household*.

Let's look at the two critical words, *father* and *son*.

Father: 'ab'

Son: 'ben'

Many rabbis have noted that *stone*, "eben', is effectively formed by overlapping 'ab' for *father*[37] and 'ben' for *son*. The place of overlap is the letter 'b', which in Hebrew is called 'beth', the *house*.

The word "eben' is therefore meant to convey an understanding that the *foundation stone* of the family is *father and son sharing the same house*.

And in case you are concerned about the ultra-masculine overtones of this word, note the gender of 'eben' is feminine, conveying the sense that the mother is the one who makes a house a home and binds parents and children together as a family.

Just as 'sekviy' unites the concept of heart with that of a shining stone tumbling from heaven, "eben' couples the concept of *foundation stone* with *a unity of father and son*. There is no separation in Jewish thinking of spiritual and material. They are not divisible into separate realms: a physical object can be the manifestation of a spiritual reality.

In fact, first the natural, then the spiritual is the principle articulated by Paul in 1 Corinthians 15:46.

We find the concept of 'sekviy' hidden deep within an incident involving Jesus which was witnessed by Peter, James and John. Fortunately, Peter wrote about that incident or we might still miss its more profound overtones.

At the transfiguration of Jesus, the radiant heartstone of a 'sekviy' was made manifest. Father and Son appear in the same 'house'. A threshold covenant occurs just six days after a name covenant: Simon had given Jesus the name 'Messiah' and, in exchange, Jesus named him Cephas, *the cornerstone, the threshold stone*.

Cephas, the living cornerstone, was bemused and bewildered at the time by the radiance of Jesus the Cornerstone as well as by God's midwife speech. However he got it later: not only do Peter's epistles talk about living stones but he quotes the one Scripture that drives straight to the heart of threshold covenant, Isaiah 28:16.

Behold I am laying in Zion for a foundation, a stone, a tested stone, a precious cornerstone of a sure foundation: 'He who believes will not be in haste.' (RSV)

The unveiling of a foundation stone on a building is an important ceremonial occasion. A modern foundation stone is not the same as the cornerstone—which was the very first stone laid of an ancient house or of the gates of a city. The doorway built over the cornerstone was a place of sacrifice—often, given the importance of city gates, human sacrifice.

The cornerstone basically formed an altar—where threshold covenants were solemnised. When a guest was expected, a host would slaughter an animal and paint its blood on the doorposts and lintels of a house as a sign of welcome. The visitor had a choice of 'passing over' the blood which had dripped onto the cornerstone or else trampling on the stone. In the first instance, he signified his willingness to accept the invitation into covenant and, in the second, he rejected it. Once the host and the guest had covenanted together, they were obligated to defend each other—even to the death.

The ceremonies involving foundation stones of modern buildings no longer have such significant overtones. However, remnants of the ancient rites persist. The red carpet, for instance, was an adaptation of the blood-stained cornerstone. Originally used to welcome an important dignitary from another country, it was a symbol intended to say, 'As you walk across this carpet at our invitation, know that while you are in our country we will defend you as if you are one of us. We will keep all the obligations of threshold covenant. We will feast with you, honour you and keep you safe. This red carpet tells you that you need have no fear.'

Of course, these days the significance is lost as Hollywood celebrities use it as a kind of parade ground.

Half-forgotten as these vestigial threshold symbols are, they are still held in high esteem. It should be no surprise to find they have important ceremonial aspects in religion, family, nations and national identity. They come in different guises and remind us of truths we have forgotten.

Many Māori families have a 'taonga', a treasured greenstone, as the heart and soul of the family home—buried beneath its foundations. One of the legends of greenstone, not surprisingly, is that of a star which swam a heavenly river before falling to earth, plunging into the ocean and eventually heaving itself up to form the land of greenstone—the South Island of New Zealand.

Islam has a foundation stone set in the corner of the Kaaba and it is almost certainly a meteorite. During the Hajj many pilgrims kiss the black stone. The stone dates back to pre-Islamic days and is alleged to have originally been associated with worship of a mother goddess.

In 205 BC, in response to terrifying showers of stones dropping out of the sky, the Roman Senate sent for a conical meteorite known as the Needle of Cybele. Cybele was a mother goddess worshipped in Asia Minor, apparently as a black skystone. The timing seems to suggest the Senate was responding to the impact event in southern Germany at Chiemgau and Tüttensee. The religion of Rome may have been polytheistic but its earliest days were dominated by worship of a stone.

The ancient religion of Egypt also had numerous examples of benbens, worshipped as foundation stones. Look carefully at the name and note its similarity to Hebrew "eben'.

The stone of Scone, also called the Stone of Destiny, was for centuries an essential part of the coronation ceremony inaugurating the reign of a new monarch of England. The story of this sandstone block is an intricate one, going back through the mists of time to the Lia Fail of Ireland. That in turn was claimed to be the stone pillow Jacob laid his head on at Bethel, when he dreamed of a ladder[38] dropping down from heaven and angels ascending and descending on it.

The "eben ha-shetiyah'—*the stone from which the world was woven*, the very foundation stone of creation with God's divine name engraved on it—was once understood to be located in the Holy of Holies in the Temple at Jerusalem. The High Priest, entering the sanctuary on the Day of Atonement, would put his fire-pan on it.

Afraid that bold and careless young men would learn the divine Name and use it to destroy the world, the sages stationed two bronze lions on iron pillars on either side of the door leading into the Holy of Holies. If anyone entered and learned the divine Name, these lions would so terrify him as he left, that the Name would be driven from his mind and forgotten.

The "eben ha-shetiyah' is still said to be at the Muslim-controlled Temple Mount in Jerusalem. The golden Dome of the Rock—the rock being the "eben ha-shetiyah' in Jewish understanding—was built over it.

Whether Māori or Roman, Egyptian, Islamic or Hebrew, these heaven-sent stones are treasured, revered, sometimes worshipped, always related back to the beginning of a structure. That structure could be family line—that is, after all, the sense of "eben', father and son in the same house.

It can also be a human being:

'*You knit me together* [sakak: weave together] *in my mother's womb*,' Psalm 139 says. '*I am fearfully and wonderfully made... Your eyes saw my unformed body* [golem: stones[39]]; *all the days ordained for me were written in your book before one of them came to be.*'

The psalm reveals each of us has a foundation stone—a threshold stone, a cornerstone, an inmost frame—call-it-what-you-will, it's the kernel of our being, our heartstone, our sekviy. It's supposed to be as radiant as a star.

It comes with a name, a calling, an inheritance, a promise of destiny.

On it is an inscription that proclaims our belonging—personally and corporately; as an individual and as a family. The name there should be Jesus—with perhaps a tiny asterisk and accompanying footnote: 'of Nazareth'.

My problem was that my sekviy, my heartstone, had a very different inscription: some Celtic god named Nuada.

I was conducting a seminar on name covenants when a woman came up to me and asked about a name she'd invented for her son. Would the name have any meaning or was it just random sounds? How could anyone determine where its dedication, if any, lay? What inscription would be on the cornerstone? Would there be any chance of her son discovering his true calling?

Now these were all very theoretical questions. And, I pointed out, my best guess would still be a guess. She told me the invented name and added that the only word she'd ever found remotely like it was Welsh.

'That could be the meaning,' I said when she explained her discovery. 'But actually your son's name sounds much closer to the Welsh version of Merlin.' In my quest to discover what *heartstone* meant I'd frequently butted up against legends of Merlin and King Arthur, so I knew a reasonable amount about the name variants.

A moment of deathly silence followed while the woman stared at me as if I'd looked suddenly into her soul.

'Three days before my son was born,' she said, obviously shocked, 'I had an incredibly vivid dream about Merlin. It came out of nowhere. It was so striking I still remember it. But I've hardly thought of it until this moment.'

The question is: did the dream really come out of nowhere?

As Isaac and Rebecca named their son *Deceiver* for the unresolved spiritual issue descending from Abraham, do we choose names highlighting the unresolved spiritual issues of our family lines?

'The heartstone of the problem is Nuada,' God said to me.

It was years before finally dawned on me He didn't say, 'The heartstone of *your* problem is Nuada.'

It's *the* problem, not *my* problem. This dilemma is not unique to me.

'Tikkun Olam' is the Jewish way of saying: 'the world needs fixing, and it's our job to fix it.' In the words of the Talmud: 'It is not upon you to finish the work, but you are not free to ignore it.'

Mishna, *Ethics*

When I was twelve I fell off my bike and broke my wrist. It was in plaster for months. During that time I experienced a nightmare so vivid that it didn't stop even when I woke up. The dream was about one of my arms turning to metal.

At school we were doing a science experiment to produce hydrogen gas by pouring acid onto zinc. I was fascinated by the zinc. It was the same bright silver colour as my arm in the nightmare; the same cold glinting hardness. True silver was softer and greyer and had a warmer feel.

The nightmare grew so intense and so regular that I'd flail out of it, sure my entire arm had turned to zinc and that spirals of metal were creeping up my face. Even fully awake, the sensation would remain—sometimes for hours—and I'd have to check a mirror regularly to make sure I was still flesh and blood.

It would be all too easy to attribute the nightmare to the pain of my broken wrist and my plaster-covered arm. But the onset of this dream had been years beforehand—the accident simply intensified it; it didn't start it.

By the time the plaster was removed, the arm-turning-to-metal nightmare had become coupled with a dream about a tsunami as high as heaven. And although the first dream faded, the second didn't. It went on for several more years before it too dissipated.

Now when God first spoke to me, saying, 'The heartstone of the problem is Nuada,' I hadn't thought of these nightmares in well over thirty years.

But the details came back with a rush when I realised that the legend of Nuada involved the replacement of a silver hand for a flesh-and-blood one. I also realised that something about Nuada of the Silver Hand had to be lodged deep in my psyche because the first two children's fantasies I'd written both had significant references to silver hands in their first chapters.

People often tell me they don't remember any of their dreams—let alone their recurring dreams. I have two suggestions: first, pray about remembering. If you still don't recall them—and, for some people, prayer is enough to unlock the memory—then second, sit down and write a fantasy or a fairytale. Don't put any restraints on your imagination. Let it run free. Don't censor what's coming out. I'd be very surprised if the exercise did not reveal and identify who has legal right to your threshold stone.[40]

How did Nuada of the Silver Hand, of whom I'd never heard as a child, come to assert legal right in my life at twelve years of age?

Threshold covenants in Scripture are always linked to name

covenants. Yes, it was about my name. It was about breaking an ancestral covenant with a spirit who was far from happy I spent my time talking to the God of the Hebrews, entirely ignoring the Celtic pantheon.

Of course, breaking a covenant means that, whatever curses were invoked when the covenant was first inaugurated, are liable to descend on the covenant-violator. The fact that the inauguration of the covenant was centuries ago is quite irrelevant. Covenants don't have an end-date. They are an ongoing binding tie that exists as long as the family endures; they survive the death of those who took them out; they involve lines of inheritance in a perpetual stream—and they keep doing this, until someone decides to take action to revoke them. And if someone rises up to do that, then they'd better have another—and more powerful—covenant defender lined up to protect them against the onslaught of curses about to overtake them.

A name is an integral part of a covenant.

In the past few centuries, we've become convinced that most names are derived from occupations or from locations. We forget that almost all occupations had their own guilds and gods; while localities had their own 'genius loci'—the spirit of a place.

God Himself places His own name in Israel.

And anything that He does, the satan copies. Or at least tries to. The satan does not have a name but he's stolen plenty, claimed them for his own and demanded allegiance because, at some point, someone has recognised his claim.

When God gave Adam sovereignty over naming, his free will meant he could give away these privileges.

God stripped the satan of his name and cast him out of heaven for trading in names[41] and he's been trying to get as many back as he can ever since, to usurp the identity, destiny, inheritance and power embodied in them.

Ori, my brother in the island mode,
In every tongue and meaning much my friend,
This story of your country and your clan,
In your loved house, your too much honoured guest,
I made in English. Take it, being done;
And let me sign it with the name you gave.
Teriitera.

Robert Louis Stevenson,
The Song of Rahéro

Name covenants still existed well into the nineteenth century. They were particularly prevalent across the Pacific islands and within the indigenous cultures of Australia and Nuigini. In December 1888, Fanny Stevenson, wife of the author of *Treasure Island* and *Kidnapped*, wrote from Tautira in Tahiti, describing her husband's name exchange with Ori a Ori, a local chief.

Princess Moë apparently conveyed Stevenson's request for the exchange to Ori, who responded with an offer of brotherhood: 'So now, if you please, Louis is no more Louis, having given that name away in the Tahitian form of Rui, but is known as Terii-Tera.'

Fanny revealed that Terii-Tera was Ori's first name, 'Ori of Ori' being his clan name. Very soon the covenant obligations became evident: Stevenson's yacht was shipwrecked and Rui (formerly Ori, but now using the Tahitian form of Louis as his name) came to the rescue.

'You are my brother: all that I have is yours.' Rui's words, his actions in providing taro and shelter, and his voyage through a raging storm to Pape'ete to acquire English food for his guests, demonstrates the obligation he felt due to the name exchange. His words express the ancient Hebrew concept of covenant.

Captain James Cook made advantageous use of name exchanges

during his Pacific voyages: just like Stevenson, he made a name exchange in Tahiti with another Ori. In the Hawaiian Islands, he exchanged names in a 'pili aiki' ceremony with Kalani'ōpu'u. Gifts were also swapped: a feather helmet and feather cloaks—symbols of rank— for a linen shirt and a sword.

Kalani'ōpu'u's covenantal action might have been lost on the English sailors but it is clear the chieftain understood his commitment. Years later, an attempt to take him hostage to secure the return of a longboat led to Cook's death at the hands of enraged islanders. But Kalani'ōpu'u mourned the loss of his English brother.

Such name covenant exchanges are so important in the Pacific they naturally have special terminology attached to them. 'Pili aiki' in Hawaii, 'kaboara' in Kiribati, 'e inoa' in the Marquessan islands, 'tayo' throughout Polynesia and 'natam' in the Torres Strait.

Over in the Caribbean islands of the Antilles, a name covenant is termed 'guaitiao'.

In the early days of Australian settlement, many name exchanges are recorded—including that of the first governor, Arthur Phillip, with the indigenous luminary, Woollarawarre Bennelong. Bennelong was known as 'Governor' while Phillip became 'Woollarawarre'.

English writers consistently remark on the custom as one of the highest friendship and deepest esteem, but fail to note its origin in the cutting of covenant[42] or recognise its Biblical overtones. They present it as charming but primitive, not recognising it as one of the 'ancient paths' Jeremiah laments have passed from common knowledge. Although the concept of name covenant had disappeared within the sphere of Western ideas, European exposure to it continued on through these journeys to the South Seas. But its fading was inevitable, once covenant became confused with contract rather than oneness.

Remnants of the notion of name covenant only linger today in the tendency of women to take their husband's name on marriage. Remnants of threshold covenant remain there too—in the tradition of a groom carrying his bride across the threshold. Lest she should dash

35

her foot against a stone.

The other vestige of threshold covenant is, strangely enough, the free hospital. In my home state of Queensland, the hallowed tradition of a free public hospital system has been fought over, but miraculously preserved, through countless political swings and changes of government.

The root of the word *hospital* is *hospitality*.

A threshold covenant was originally a covenant based in hospitality.

The original sense of 'hospital' was simply a *guest house* or *inn*. The word started to acquire its modern meaning as a place for the sick about a thousand years ago. The Order of Knights of the Hospital of Saint John of Jerusalem, commonly called 'The Hospitallers', began caring for sick, injured and poverty-stricken pilgrims to the Holy Land in their guest house.

The Hospitallers as a Europe-wide brotherhood did not survive the Reformation. However, the words 'hospice' and 'hospital' had been so long associated with the Knights' activities that their meanings changed irrevocably from *guest* house to house *of the sick*. Another threshold covenant notion that did not survive long after the Reformation is the church as a place of asylum. Accused men were once able to flee to a sanctuary and would be safe from any pursuit the moment they stepped over the boundary.

That extraordinarily beautiful notion—the church as a place of refuge, reflecting God as our one true refuge—has vanished long ago.

Men have sometimes exchanged names with their friends, as if they would signify that in their friend each loved his own soul.

Ralph Waldo Emerson

There was one identity, destiny, inheritance and power the satan wanted more than any other. That of Jesus.

Had he got it, the satan could have over-written the inscription on the foundation stone of the entire cosmos, re-directing it to himself. He tried hard. He tried very hard.

In the stories of the three temptations Jesus faces, it's easy to miss the allusions to the cornerstone, the threshold covenant, and the name of God.

In Luke's record, the devil takes Jesus to the highest point of the Temple for the last test before His ministry starts.[43] The location, in combination with the words uttered by the satan, indicates the true significance of the test. Every threshold requires a sacrifice and, here, the satan as the threshold guardian, demands it of Jesus. As a former covering cherub, the satan is uniquely qualified to usurp the place of the holy cherubim and to quote from Psalm 91:

'If you are the Son of God, throw yourself down. For it is written: He will command His angels concerning you, and they will lift You up in their hands, so that You will not strike your foot against a stone.'

Matthew 4:6 NIV

The verse alludes to a refusal of a threshold covenant. When a host invited a guest to come into covenant with him, the visitor could accept or decline. To accept, the guest would 'pass over' the blood-stained threshold stone. To refuse, the guest would 'trample on', 'dash' or 'strike' his foot against the stone. That was, naturally, an insult.

Psalm 91:12 speaks of angelic protection to ensure a refusal does not even occur accidentally. The very next verse from Psalm 91 is threshold-saturated: *'You will tread on the lion and the cobra; you will trample the great lion and the serpent.'*

A closer look at this verse reveals:
Lion: 'shachal'
Cobra: 'pethen'
Young lion: 'kephiyr'
Serpent: 'tanniyn'

The Hebrew word, 'pethen', translated *cobra*, is one possible source of English *python*. From 'pethen' comes 'miphtan', always translated *threshold*. However, from its context, I consider 'miphtan' is better rendered *defiled threshold*.

Young lion, 'kephiyr', is also threshold-related. It's from 'kaphar', *atonement* or *covering*. From it, in turn, words like *ransom, reconciliation, forgiveness, mercy-seat, cornerstone* and *threshold stone* are derived.

Adding to the threshold overtones of the verse, 'shachal' may well pun on 'shachar', *dawn*—the threshold of the day.

The serpent, 'tanniyn', often translated *dragon* may refer to Leviathan or Nehushtan. The last syllable of each of these is *serpent*. Leviathan is the fire-breathing serpent described in Job, as well as a spirit of twisting and backlash. It's no coincidence, in my view, that it shares part of its name with Levi. Just as the tribe of Levi was called to minister before the Lord in the Temple court, so I consider Leviathan a fallen seraph whose office was to minister in the heavenly court, defending the honour of God.

Nehushtan was a bronze serpent, raised up by Moses in the wilderness to heal anyone bitten by deadly snakes. It later was kept in the Temple where it became an idol. As a consequence, it was destroyed during the reform which occurred in the reign of King Hezekiah.

This subtle evocation of the Holy of Holies within the Temple is reinforced by the mention of the lions. According to ancient tradition, bronze lions guarded the entrance to the Holy of Holies, specifically to guard the name of God inscribed on the Foundation Stone.

This is what the temptation is all about. And it's why it doesn't occur in the desert but on the pinnacle of the Temple.

The satan isn't simply asking Jesus to throw Himself off the roof and test God's promises. He's asking Jesus to abuse His covenant with the Father. Not to reject it, just bend it a little. Pervert it.

Fat chance, you may think. However, the Book of Judges tells us otherwise. It's a compendium of short stories about how the Israelites played fast and loose with threshold covenants—keeping the letter of the agreement while mangling its spirit.

By tempting Jesus to pervert His covenant with God, the satan clearly wanted access to the Holy of Holies, to the sacred Name and all the power that went with it. He wanted to install his own unholy threshold guardians—Python, Rachab and Leviathan—in the sanctuary.

Two of these guardians are mentioned directly in Psalm 91 within a series of promises from God relating to threshold-crossing. But those promises, as evidenced by verse 12, only hold true for those who have not refused His covenant. It's for those who have a godly, not ungodly, inscription on their sekviy.

In fact, often the very word in Greek for *ungodly* Paul uses is 'bebelos'—from 'belos', *threshold*. *Ungodly* has the connotation of trampling on the threshold and refusing covenant with the Lord.

Like 'miphtan', 'belos' has a sense of being a defiled threshold, not a clean one. That's because 'belos' is also the word for *darts* or *arrows*, as in the *fiery darts* directed against us mentioned in Ephesians 6:16.

Jesus faced incredible opposition from the satan as He approached the threshold into His calling.

He tackled the situation with forty days of prayer and fasting. On the threshold itself, He displayed supreme caution. So why have we got this idea the door into our calling is going to open smoothly and effortlessly? Why do we think it'll be plain sailing all the way, the mountains levelled and the valleys filled in to make our passage into our destiny and inheritance a slick, easy ride?

Is it because we think we have a covenant defender in Jesus Himself? A highly significant verse regarding threshold covenant, Isaiah 28:16, is flanked on both sides by cautions about such thinking. We don't get a threshold covenant with Jesus unless we've got rid of our false refuges, our shelter of lies and the accompanying covenants with death.

You boast, 'We have entered into a covenant with death... we have made a lie our refuge and falsehood our hiding place.' So this is what the Sovereign Lord says: 'See, I lay a stone in Zion... a precious cornerstone for a sure foundation; the one who relies on it will never be stricken with panic... hail will sweep away your refuge, the lie, and water will overflow your hiding place. Your covenant with death will be annulled...'

Isaiah 28:15-18 NIV

Therein lies the problem most of us fail to recognise. We think we have a covenant with Jesus. But we've simply got a relationship. A non-exclusive one at that. One that also includes entities like Nuada.

3

The Xarama

THE EXTRAORDINARY POWER OF THRESHOLD COVENANTS is evident in Peter's testimony about the Transfiguration:

He received from God the Father honour and glory when such a voice came to Him from the Excellent Glory: 'This is My beloved Son, in whom I am well pleased.' And we heard this voice which came from heaven when we were with Him on the holy mountain.

2 Peter 1:17-18 NKJV

None of the gospel writers identify the 'holy mountain'. Some scholars believe it's Mount Tabor in Galilee; I believe it's Mount Hermon in the north. The highest mountain in Israel, Hermon has formed a boundary with other nations since ancient times; at present it borders both Lebanon and Syria. From its slopes flow the headwaters of the Jordan river—waters that eventually reach the lowest point on earth. The course of the Jordan to the Dead Sea effectively forms a continuation of the Great Rift Valley of Africa. Mount Hermon is close to the northern terminus of this astonishing geological feature that is visible even from the moon.

Geographically therefore it is a threshold place.

Snow and frost usually remain on its highest peaks even in summer; it is the first place in Israel to receive the light of the sun each day. The first covenant Abram cut with God—the blood covenant—is believed to have taken place on the slopes of Mount Hermon.

Chronologically therefore it is a threshold place.

In ancient Israelite understanding, it was apparently synonymous with the *north*, 'zaphon'. On Mount Zaphon, a titanic struggle between the monstrous Typhon and the chief of the gods occurred. In different ages, that chief god had differing names. From Typhon comes the word *typhoon* with its influences on *python*.[44]

Since one of the Hebrew words for *threshold* is derived from the word for *python*, etymologically it is a threshold place.[45]

According to the Book of Enoch, Mount Hermon was the place the fallen angels first alighted on earth. Here they threw curses at each other—making a pact that bears resemblance to a covenant ceremony.

Traditionally therefore it is a threshold place.

In Canaanite legend, Zaphon was the place where the gods held their assembly—where they met in council. To fulfil the prophecy of Psalm 82, Jesus had to stand up in the 'assembly of the gods' at some point. This is why I believe Mount Hermon is far more probable as the location of the Transfiguration: to challenge the seventy members of Divine Council, it's where He naturally had to go. On His descent, He immediately commissioned seventy disciples to preach the arrival of the kingdom of heaven, thereby setting up His own version of this Council. This action confirms the location for me.

Because Mount Hermon fulfilled so many threshold criteria—both of heaven and hell—it's the most logical place for Jesus to undertake a threshold covenant with Peter, James and John as representatives of the yet-to-be-born church.

It was only six days previously that Peter had still been called Simon. Less than a week before, he had received his new name, Hebrew 'Cephas' or Greek 'Petros'. Cephas means *threshold stone* or *cornerstone*; Peter has overtones in both Hebrew and Greek. From Greek its usual translation is *rock* but more fully it's *a rock from which an enterprise is started*. In Hebrew, Peter means *firstborn, the one who opens the way*.

A name that fits either language, Greek or Hebrew, Peter has a sense of *openings, thresholds, beginnings*.

As *God's Pottery* indicates, the time between a name covenant and a threshold covenant repeatedly given in Scripture is six days. This has a parallel in human gestation. If the fertilised egg of conception (a name covenant being God's whisper which creates the soul, paving the way for conception at that moment) is not implanted in the womb in six days, then it will naturally abort. A threshold covenant is an implantation; if one does not occur within six days, the name covenant will not 'take'. The new destiny and identity which are encoded in the new name will miscarry.

No wonder the words of God at the Transfiguration were those of a midwife.[46]

Jesus the Cornerstone created a new cornerstone for His church which is both Himself and not Himself. He created it on Mount Hermon when He should have created it, as Isaiah prophesied, in Zion.

Thus says the Lord God, 'Behold, I lay in Zion for a foundation a stone, a tried stone, a precious cornerstone of sure foundation: he who believes shall not be in haste.'

Isaiah 28:16 HNV

Yet while Mount Hermon is *not* Zion, it is also covenantally Zion. Its oldest Hebrew name is Sion and the prophetic words of Psalm 133 proclaim the unity of Sion and Zion—north and south meeting in beauty and holiness. True brotherhood, the psalm declares, is like the dew of Hermon dripping like anointing oil on the high priest in the temple in Jerusalem.

Hermon is where the first light of morning touches on the land of Israel. Peter's commentary on his experience of the Transfiguration concludes: '*And so we have the prophetic word confirmed, which you do well to heed as a light that shines in a dark place, until the day dawns and the morning star rises in your hearts.*'

Paul in Romans 13:12 reveals this is the time to put on the armour of light. Because thresholds are peculiarly dangerous places.

Dawn and sunset see stars... in a blue sky; but morning... and afternoon do not, poor things.

Elizabeth Goudge

I listened recently to an audio-presentation by a speaker who said he wasn't a morning person. He admitted, as if claiming membership of a very exclusive club, that he'd never seen a dawn.

I was seriously taken aback by his attitude. Obviously he didn't realise what he was missing.

I regularly get up early enough to watch the dawn. Ever since I realised Paul was making some profoundly complex statement about daybreak when he discussed the armour of light in Romans 13, I've taken an interest in the transitions that occur around sunrise.

As I grope towards understanding the nature of Greek 'xarama' and Hebrew 'shachar', I recognise how important it is to observe daybreak. I'm not sure the connection Peter makes about the Transfiguration and sunrise could ever get beyond the theoretical in my heart if I'd never watched the dawn unveil its threshold mysteries.

'Xarama' and 'shachar' are not strictly words for *dawn*. 'Xarama' is the Greek word for *the time just before sunrise*. Its Hebrew equivalent, 'shachar', can be translated as either *darkness* or *dawn*.[47]

The period just before dawn is difficult to describe. Some people use the word twilight but, at least where I live, there's no suffusion of gold-dust limning the air. It's truly a time when it's impossible to decide if it's dark or light. From my window the coming of dawn is a slow and majestic pageant: the eastern horizon turns from indigo to royal purple, then a shore of vivid orange appears before a lemon wash abruptly covers an entire quadrant of sky. As a lip of the sun peeps over the horizon, grey clouds blush peach-pink and shafts of light spill upwards while the sky fades to pale blue.

The signal of change is the pale lemon wash. It has none of the velvet richness of night, none of the dramatic rose-coloured radiance that heralds the sun reaching the horizon. Instead, it's like a thin veneer of palest yellow making a brief appearance on stage before being shooed off unceremoniously by the main act. This is the point when the stars disappear: the glitter of the morning star fades into the wash. The temperature begins to drop sharply as ground dew takes heat from the air to evaporate.

I don't know whether the 'xarama' is the same everywhere else in the world. I'm probably describing just the sub-tropical version. But one thing I am sure of: it's a complex event. It's a threshold, after all.

The sophistication of the transition from night to day is demonstrated by the fact 'shachar' can also be translated as *significance* or *meaning* or *soul*.

The imagery of the soul and the pre-dawn breath of God is exactly what Paul uses in his lead-up to an important admonition: '...*the night is far gone, the day is at hand. Let us therefore cast off the works of darkness and put on the armour of light...*' (Romans 13:12 NRS)

As I have pointed out in *God's Panoply*, divine armour is the punchline of a sequence of thought that Paul covers twice in his letters— in Ephesians and Romans. In both cases he begins with a command to submit, moves on to counsel his readers about loving relationships and finishes with an exhortation to put on some kind of divine armour.

Here Paul says that, as the day emerges from night, we should put on the armour of light. He's describing the hour of 'xarama' or 'shachar'. There's another Hebrew word for this period of time: 'nesheph', from 'nashaph', *to blow*, a variant[48] of 'naphash', *breath* or *refresh*.

As we have seen in the previous chapter, God's breath kisses us into life by naming us and thus giving us a soul. Hence why 'shachar' means both *pre-dawn* and *soul*.

The creation of a soul is like the sun coming up.

It's no coincidence that the creation of a soul is through the act of giving a name, and the word for *sun* in Hebrew, 'shemesh', is basically *name fire*.

A name fires up our souls, kindles our calling, and ignites our identity.

And we need the armour of light, or else the armour of God, because without it, we'll be doused down and our light extinguished by the opposition. We're supposed to be the light of the world, a city set on a hill, a lamp shining in the darkness—but, unprepared for the threshold, we are often reduced to barely glowing embers. Sometimes, the spirits of the threshold have had such a field day with us, we're not even embers—we're ash.

But, never forget, our Lord is the one who trades beauty for ashes.

The soul can split the sky in two and let the face of God shine through.
Edna St. Vincent Millay

Thresholds are potentially deadly places.

Throughout myth, legend, modern fantasy, science fiction and gaming, you'll find threshold guardians aplenty. They're an archetype that is usually monstrous in nature and they test the hero at a crucial point in his journey. More often than not, they require a sacrifice from the hero in return for safe passage.

In, for example, the first-released *Star Wars* movie, Luke Skywalker is about to board the *Millennium Falcon* and make good his escape with Han Solo, Princess Leia and Chewbacca.

Luke comes out the door leading to the deck where the spacecraft is docked. Tick, threshold.

Darth Vader appears just beyond another doorway. Tick, monstrous guardian.

Darth Vader and Obi Wan are engaged in a light-sabre duel, during which Obi Wan deliberately sacrifices himself. Tick, threshold sacrifice.

George Lucas framed the *Star Wars* saga around Joseph Campbell's theories about the 'Hero's Journey'. A significant element of Campbell's work looks at the perils of the threshold and the potentially fatal encounter with the threshold guardians.

The bridge is another threshold archetype: like a door, it permits passage across a perilous border into a different realm. Thus we find the monstrous firewhip-wielding Balrog guarding the Bridge of Khazad-dûm in *The Fellowship of the Ring*. And we find that Gandalf the Grey sacrifices himself on the threshold to allow the remainder of the Fellowship to escape.

In the aptly-named *Monty Python and the Holy Grail*, the concept of the terrifying bridge guardian is gleefully satirised, using a trope from the myth of Oedipus meeting the Sphinx. But instead of a hybrid creature with the body of a lion and the face of a woman,[49] the Grail-seekers from Arthur's court are met by a seedy old man.

After Sir Robin and Sir Galahad fail to answer the old man's questions, they are pitched into a volcanic abyss. King Arthur is left to face the guardian's next question: 'What is the air-speed velocity of an unladen swallow?'

Arthur, fortunately, knows enough about swallows to want clarification. 'What do you mean? An African or European swallow?'

The guardian, unable to answer, is then catapulted into the abyss himself.

Examples from popular culture as these may be, they share basic motifs: the dangerous threshold, the grotesque guardian, the threshold sacrifice.

In real life, we tend to dismiss the idea of the threshold guardian.

We tend to think of them as only occurring in movies or fantasy fiction.

But threshold guardians are not an unbiblical concept. In fact, they're extremely prevalent throughout Scripture. From the moment the cherubim are introduced as guarding the gates of Eden with their killer swords, the concept of exceedingly scary, highly dangerous threshold sentinels is apparent. In case you haven't noticed that angels, holy or unholy, are very scary, I'd like to point out that heaven obviously has a protocol for human-angelic encounters. It starts with the words: 'Do not be afraid.'

Other threshold moments where angels appear: the tomb of Joseph of Arimethea, just after the Resurrection. (John 20:11-12) As the firstfruits of those raised from the dead, Jesus passed over a previously impassable boundary. His threshold crossing created a new frontier for the whole of humanity.

Forty days later, another[50] pair of angels was present as Jesus left to return to heaven. As He ascended to cross this significant threshold, they chided the disciples for staring at an empty sky. (Acts 1:10)

Spiritual thresholds are not just endings, they can also be beginnings. When Jesus was about to start His ministry, angels came to comfort Him after His testing in the wilderness.

Three more significant thresholds occurred around the miracle of Jesus' birth. It had been prophesied that a man with the spirit of Elijah would come before the Messiah would appear. An angel appeared to the husband of Mary's cousin Elizabeth to advise him of the coming birth of John the Baptist. Gabriel, that same angel, appeared to announce to Mary she had been chosen as the mother of the Messiah.

Around five hundred years previously, Gabriel had also appeared as a messenger to the prophet Daniel. Again it was a threshold moment. The time had come for the Jewish people to return to their homeland. The seventy years of exile that the prophet Jeremiah had foretold were up and the doorway of freedom should have been wide open. But it wasn't. Although a decree had gone out from God in answer to Daniel's prayer, the opposition in the heavenlies was fierce.

Gabriel battled twenty-one days to get through to Daniel. Only the angel Michael came to his aid.

Sometimes the only way we can really recognise a threshold is by the intensity of the opposition we face.

The reason angelic forces like Gabriel and Michael appear at thresholds is to protect a new move of God against the powers that would destroy it at its most vulnerable.

But the fact remains: sometimes the hosts of God aren't there to protect us as we try to come into our calling. When we have a threshold covenant with another god, they do not have the legal right to fully protect us.

A threshold covenant with another god means there's something terribly amiss with our personal cornerstone. Our sekviy has been tainted.

Our threshold stone is a 'miphtan', not a 'kaph'.

As mentioned previously, 'kaph' relates to a threshold stone with a shallow basin carved into it. This hollow catches the blood dripping from the lintels and doorposts to welcome an expected guest. Because 'kaph' is so intimately connected with the sacrifice solemnising the threshold covenant, it is associated with words like 'kippur', *atonement*, and 'kaphowr', *covering*.

Now a 'miphtan' is also a threshold. English translations unfortunately make no distinction between a 'miphtan' and a 'kaph'. However even a cursory examination of the use of 'miphtan' shows it only occurs when a *defiled* threshold is described.

The first use of 'miphtan' occurs in 1 Samuel 5:4 when, in the presence of the Ark of the Covenant, the statue of the fish-god Dagon crashes and breaks on the threshold of a Philistine temple. 'Miphtan' also occurs all through Ezekiel's vision of God's departure from the temple in Jerusalem. Since Ezekiel had previously detailed the spiritual corruption of the priests and their desecration of the sanctuary, it is clear these thresholds are defiled ones.[51]

Significantly 'miphtan' is derived from the Hebrew word, 'pethen', *python*.

By making no distinction between 'kaph' and 'miphtan' in translation, our English versions of the Scriptures occlude the fact that the Hebrew people always knew the spirit of constriction was symptomatic of a defiled threshold.

And they also clearly knew Python did not work alone.

The threshold experience has its own language. Listen closely and the vocabulary is obvious. It's also instinctive—because most people have never heard of threshold guardians nor are they aware of their distinctive character.

Cate, a champion athlete and world record-holder, swam so badly at a significant sporting event that she described her performance as the 'greatest choke'.

Pete described his inability to sell his long-standing, profitable store so that he could move into the full-time ministry he'd always dreamed of as feeling like he was in the 'grip of a boa constrictor'.

Chris described his experience with a manager who interviewed him three times, then spent a week showing him round while giving him intimate and detailed explanations of the inner workings of the company as 'slow strangulation' when the position was re-advertised.

Bronwyn just finished a course in chaplaincy when her mother became seriously ill and she had to care for her. A few years later she was finally able to take on the role she'd trained for, but she felt 'squeezed out' of any opportunities she might have had.

When people start using terms like 'choked', 'constricted', 'strangled', 'squeezed', 'pressured', 'smothered', 'squashed', 'crushed', 'wrung out', 'constrained', 'restricted'—especially in regard to passing over a threshold—then it's clear Python is at work.

On the other hand, when people start using terms like 'wasted', 'ruined', 'trashed', 'wrecked', 'spread thin', 'disintegrated', then it's more likely Rachab is at work.

The natural temptation is to bind such spirits, revile them, and demand or command them to leave. Should we fall into this temptation—and go further than saying, as the angel Michael did, 'The Lord rebuke you!'—then we become prey for Leviathan.

The fruit of the Spirit overcomes all these powers. And, *if* it doesn't, then it's time to look at what kind of fruit it is. My unregenerate, fleshly love can do no more to evict these cosmic entities than the splash of a single raindrop can clean up a massive ocean oil spill.

But the true, sacrificial agápē flowing from below the Father's throne and mediated by the cross of Jesus can scatter each and every one of them at His direction.

Cherubim and seraphim: the angel hosts of God. They have specific roles and offices. The cherubim guard the doorways, admitting no one who is unrighteous. The seraphim proclaim the honour and holiness of God.

These roles are counterfeited by the cohorts of the satan. It's easy for them to do because they retain their offices—the gifts of God being irrevocable. We should be escorted across the threshold into our true calling by guardian angels. Instead, as so often happens, we are squeezed by Python, spread thin by Rachab and, if we should manage to get a toehold in the doorway, whiplashed by Leviathan.

To get across the threshold, these sentinels want us to offer them a sacrifice. And lots of people make the choice to give them one.

Some people choose to sacrifice another person. It might be a relationship with a spouse, a partnership with business associate, the future prospects of a child or a friend.

Some people choose to sacrifice themselves. They self-sabotage as they reach the threshold, often in bizarre, inexplicable ways.

Some people choose to sacrifice the honour of God or the possibility of giving glory to His name. They conceal their faith—often with the stated intention of positioning themselves for even greater witness in the future.

Some people choose to recognise that Jesus is, in fact, the all-sufficient sacrifice to pass over the threshold into the calling God has for them. But these people are rare. So very, very rare.

The inscription written on our hearts is hidden in deep and secret darkness. We really don't have any idea what choice we'll make until those hellish gatekeepers step out abruptly in front of us and make their demands.

We don't have any idea what god's name forms the dedication on our sekviy because we're been told not to worry about nightmares, to ignore what happens in dreams, to seek professional help if we start seeing things. 'The heartstone of the problem is Nuada,' God told me.

I had no idea He was revealing a 'seal'.

Or that you need to deal with the spirit guarantors of the original covenant, revoke association with them in a courteous fashion and ask God to straighten out the perversions they've created.

Many people have been given to cursing, reviling and insulting the satan and his colleagues. Some churches have advocated this practice in their prayer meetings. This is to set intercessors up and lead them into a trap.

Peter described such activity as 'arrogant' (2 Peter 2:10) and says people will be paid back for the harm they have done (2 Peter 2:13). Jude corroborates Peter's caution and also adds that, regardless of slanderous accusation, the most the archangel Michael was willing to do when contending with the satan was say: 'The Lord rebuke you!'

When payback hits—sometimes lashing both ourselves and our families—a plea of innocence is invalid. A plea of ignorance is valid—but that's as far as it goes. We can't even ask God to forbid Leviathan paying us back for these acts of dishonour. That would violate His Word as given to us by both Peter and Jude.

But, if we've passed over the threshold—if, like Abraham, we're in that space where we can negotiate with God on behalf of others—then we can ask for minimisation of the retaliation. Or, if significant reprisal has already occurred, we can ask Him to declare, 'Enough!'

Even if we haven't passed the threshold, we can get closer to it by admitting our arrogance, admitting how deep our ignorance of our own arrogance is, repenting of using the Satan's own tactics against him and asking for God's mercy.

And while we're there, talking to God about dishonour, it's a good thing to take the opportunity to confess our dishonour of Him, of our parents, of our partner, of our children, of employers or employees, of anyone whom the Lord cares to bring to mind. Including ourselves. It is not so much that we dishonour ourselves as we come into mental and spiritual agreement with those do. This needs to be verbally revoked.

Having had this conversation with God, repent. Ask Him for His grace and for the power of His cross to change.

In such a way, I believe it is possible to remove Leviathan's legal rights.

Nonetheless, there's a secondary trap to avoid here. As John Sandford often said, human beings are inveterate idol-makers. We therefore have to be so careful when it comes to honour. We can't stop dishonouring others only to turn around and honour Honour so much that we honour Honour more than we honour God.

When it comes to Leviathan, two episodes form a telling comparison, illuminating its modus operandi with regard to honour. These episodes occurred, I believe, in the same historical moment: the stories of Job and Lot. The name of Abraham's nephew, Lot, means *covering*, *veil*—it's related to Lotan, *tightly wrapped* or *enveloped*.

Outside of the Scriptural record, Lotan happens to be the name of a sea monster in Canaanite religion; it means *coiled*. It is therefore equivalent to the Hebrew word, Leviathan, meaning *twisted* or *coiled*—though, possibly more accurately, *joined sea-monster*. Both Lotan and Leviathan are described in similar terms: 'fleeing serpent'[52] or 'fugitive serpent',[53] both seem to be 'wriggling' or 'twisting',[54] both have multiple heads.[55]

The tendency of Leviathan to wrap itself in coils around its prey shows us there's a relational concept linking Lot, *covering*, Lotan, *tightly wrapped*, and Leviathan, *coiling serpent*.

Because Leviathan is a guardian of honour and because Lot is a name obliquely related to it, we should expect his story to be about honour and dishonour. And that's exactly what it features. The first sign of dishonour comes when the herdsmen of Lot and Abram start quarrelling over grazing land. The conflict arises because both men became so rich in Egypt that the pasture is not sufficient for them to remain together. Abram suggests they move away from each other and gives Lot his pick of the land.

Now Abram is older and has been a father figure to Lot. The blessings God has showered on Abram have been so lavish and Lot has benefited so much by the relationship that his wealth has come to rival that of his uncle. For these reasons, Lot should have deferred to Abram. But he lifts up his eyes and sees a landscape so lush it seems comparable to the Garden of the Lord.

So Lot is drawn to a place that promises to be just like 'Eden': in the deepest of ironies it turns out to be Sodom, a city of the plain.

And not too long after—perhaps because of his wealth—he is invited to sit with the elders of the city in the gate. If he had indeed come to 'Eden', he would be sitting in the very place where the cherubim swung their flaming swords to and fro.

It is thus no coincidence a pair of cherubim eventually come to him. These angelic protectors are the guardians of thresholds. They are the attendants of El Shaddai as He visits Abraham to undertake a threshold covenant; they go on their way to Sodom to investigate the outcry to heaven about threshold covenant violation.

Now Sodom was on the eastern bank of the Jordan river; detached from the land of Canaan. It was not part of the inheritance God had pledged to give Abram. So in separating from his uncle and becoming deeply integrated into the culture of Sodom, Lot not only charted his own course but sheared away from the blessings God had promised.

After being rescued by Abram after the first 'world war'—the battle of the four kings and the five kings—he had a natural opportunity to make a break. But that was a chance he let go.

He goes back to a society steeped in dishonour.

And he is, eventually, unable to escape its defilement.

Two men arrive—cherubim in disguise, agents of judgment, officers of God's court with plenipotentiary powers. Their decisions are to be seen as those of God Himself. Perhaps Lot recognises their carriage, their bearing and the aura surrounding them as that of judges: he is, after all, a judge of Sodom. That's the significance of his right to 'sit in the gate'.

He offers the men hospitality. They accept. And in doing so, both sides also accept the mutual obligations and privileges of a threshold covenant. They are expected to defend Lot and his family to the death and Lot is likewise expected to expend every effort on their behalf. So—when the residents of Sodom surround the house and demand Lot's visitors be sent out to them, he offers them his daughters.

In doing so, the coils of dishonour that have always been wrapped around Lot start to squeeze tight. An honourable man[56] caught in an invidious situation, he seeks to save his guests from dishonour by heaping dishonour on his daughters. Dishonour on the right hand, dishonour on the left: whatever Lot's choice at this point, it's going to be worse than bad.

The story of Lot at Sodom is the archetypal example of threshold covenant defilement. It's a sharp and startling contrast with the story immediately before it of threshold covenant blessing. That's when God and Abraham share a meal together.

As Lot's choices become increasingly limited, we see Python's handiwork writ large. Still the cherubim make short work of Python with their explosive, dazzling intervention. Logically the reason they can do so is because Scripture records Lot as 'righteous'—if his judgments at the gate have been just and not self-serving, the cherubim will protect him as he escapes with his family beyond the city.

The cherubim hold office as judges on the righteousness of those wishing to pass over a threshold. They do not make decisions about honour. That's part of the task-list which falls to Leviathan.

The veil of degradation Sodom cast over the thinking of those who lived there becomes clear when Lot's daughters decide on a course of pre-meditated dishonour: they get their father drunk and then get pregnant to him. They name the children they conceive in such a way that his dishonour will be remembered in perpetuity through the tribal designations: Moab, *from my father*, and Ben-Ammi, *son of my father*.

Lot escaped the actions of Python but he was not delivered from Leviathan. He had sown dishonour—unwillingly, without a doubt; against his conscience, sure—but he'd done it. He was due to reap dishonour.

His story is not just about threshold covenants; it's about the choice encoded in his own name.

4

From Star Wars *to* the Green Knight

IF WE ESCAPE PYTHON, WE FACE LEVIATHAN. There are multiple failsafe accords the satan has put in place to ensure he gets full access to the power of your identity, destiny and calling—and you get nothing.

Even in creating these failsafe devices, the satan has no originality. He uses and perverts the threshold covenant design of heaven.

God appoints angels for the threshold, so the satan appoints his own guards.

God appoints a cornerstone to pass over, the satan places a stone to block.

God deposits the Holy Spirit and His Word as seal and surety, the satan deposits demonic guarantors and curses.

We can see these elements all in place in the most significant threshold event of all time: the Resurrection of Jesus.

The threefold guard of watch, stone and seal mentioned in Matthew 27:66 are: the Roman soldiers, the massive stone in front of the tomb and the governor's seal with its curses to deter tomb-robbers.

These were not trivial opponents and emplacements that Jesus had to face when He was raised from the dead. Alive in the tomb, having returned from hell and triumphed over Death, He still had several mortal foes and obstructions to overcome.

This is also our position on the threshold: although we are spiritually reborn, having died with Christ and been raised with Him, many of us are simply stuck in a tomb.

And although we have at our disposal everything we need to get out, we don't use any of it.

The sound barrier is a parallel in the natural world to a spiritual threshold. Early attempts to break the sound barrier (the point at which an aircraft moves from transonic to supersonic speed) often resulted in 'terminal damage' to both plane and pilot. Disruptive shock waves led to the break-up of some craft in flight; surface force on some planes was so difficult to control the pilot was unable to correct the stick, thus crashing in powered flight into terrain. Airflow between the wings and tail surfaces in some models was so severe it was impossible to pull out.

Chuck Yeager, the test pilot credited as the first to crack the sound barrier, was of the view that the buffeting might cease at higher speeds—not increase. So while others slowed down, he sped up.

Similarly, in the spiritual world, the crossing of the threshold brings us through potentially fatal turbulence to a place of calm.[57] But just as Yeager needed the right sort of plane to achieve this feat, we need the right sort of armour.

Yeager had a huge team of specialists behind him. And we're meant to have likewise. Although we've been taught to put on the Armour of God, few of us have been told that we're supposed to put it on each other. The armour is for the Body of Christ, rather than for individual use.[58]

The first item Paul exhorts us to put on each other is the belt of 'not-forgetting'. *'Stand firm then, with the belt of truth buckled around your waist...'* (Ephesians 6:14 NIV) The Greek word for *truth* in this verse is 'aletheia', from 'a-', *not*, and from Lethe, both the mythological river of forgetfulness flowing through the Underworld and the spirit of forgetfulness and oblivion.

Paul is warning us about the first and foremost of the threshold spirits: the one that ranges out from the doorway and approaches us long before we reach it. Yes, it's the spirit of forgetting. This spirit gets Hell's Efficiency Award year-in year-out. If there's a prize for the Science of Sin in the demonic world, this spirit has the top award.

Temptation is a risky business—after all, humans resist. Even people who aren't believers regularly turn their back on temptation because they hold fast to a moral code. People chained to a sinful habit can become so sickened with their own behaviour that they throw off temptation and look for help.

Temptation is therefore not an economical strategy from Hell's perspective. After all, you win some, you lose some.

Nonetheless Hell would like us to think temptation is its main strategy. That's to obscure its real one: getting us to forget. When we're traumatised by the action of another or ashamed at our own actions, it's so easy to cut a deal with the spirit of oblivion. It promises us an easy way to peace by seducing us into suppression of our memories. But:

If we've forgotten, we can't forgive.

If we've forgotten, we can't repent.

If we've forgotten, we can't renounce.

If we've forgotten, we can't reconcile.

We'll still reap what we've sown. But we'll have no idea why.

Does Paul mention any of the other threshold spirits by name? As we've seen, he uses the word 'bebelos', *ungodly*, from 'belos', meaning both *dart* and *threshold*. The derivation of 'bebelos' offers us an insight into the threshold that we might normally miss. It's an ungodly one.

The darts Paul mentions are therefore not spiritual arrows or spear-thrusts we are likely to encounter on a daily basis. I believe they are ones we can expect in an ambush as we try to cross over the threshold into our destiny and calling. It appears that 'belos' is cognate with 'miphtan' and that they genuinely have the same sense of defilement that English 'threshold' doesn't retain.

Consequently I believe Paul didn't need to mention the Python spirit by name or the vampire spirit with its stabbing stake, because his readers would have understood they were present, simply by his use of 'belos'. In addition, his use of imagery coming from the battle gear of a Roman legionnaire alludes to the need to oppose an army spirit—what I've termed the 'Janissary' in *God's Pottery*. I chose this term because 'army' does not have any connotation of an agenda to kill the father or the father's culture that 'Janissary' does. (Although there's a Biblical term I could have chosen, 'one of the spirits of Helkath-Hazzurim', it seemed too much of a mouthful to be effective.)

So with four of the seven guardians of the threshold space and the passage beyond it clearly on display in Paul's writing about the Armour of God, ancient readers would have got the picture that they're all there amongst the more generic 'principalities, powers and world rulers'.

It's unfortunate that we don't realise this passage is primarily about threshold situations. We don't recognise his allusions to the spirits of forgetting, constriction, wasting, backlash, rejection, father-destruction and vampirism.

God asked Job: '*Have you been shown the gates of death or met the janitors of shadowland?*' (Job 38:17 NJB)

One commentator calls the phrase 'janitors of shadowland' an absurdity. No! It's perfect. In one of its earliest senses, 'janitor' meant *doorkeeper*. And these threshold spirits are indeed doorkeepers of a realm of darkness and confusion. They want to feed on us—on our souls, savouring them as delicacies.[59]

They mirror the gatekeepers and doorkeepers of the Temple, which is in itself a reflection of the courts of heaven. So strong is the copying that we find a recurrence of several unusual names amongst the office-bearers of either side. Amongst the Levites who return from exile in Babylon are these doorkeepers: Akkub, Ahiman, Shallum and Talmon. The Anakim, the giants of Hebron who—at least as far as the twelve spies sent out by Moses were concerned—were the spiritual gatekeepers of Canaan, have eerily similar names: Ahiman, Sheshai and Talmai.

As Arie Uittenbogaard points out, there's a strange symmetry in these names that no commentary even hints at.

Anakim is usually translated *sons of Anak*, since the word is the plural of 'anak', the origin of our word *neck*. The name 'Anak' is generally given as *necklace* or *long-necked*, and comes from a root meaning to *strangle* or *choke*.

And if your mind flits across to the *Star Wars* saga and Anakin Skywalker who repeatedly used a technique called Force choke, it's not surprising. Nor should fans of the series be surprised to know that the parallel name amongst the Levite gatekeepers, Akkub, means *insidious*.[60]

While *Star Wars* does have a considerable number of mythic references to the threshold, there is a story that far out-classes it. This is *The Silver Chair* by CS Lewis, the author of the seven-book children's fantasy series, *The Chronicles of Narnia*.

Here Python appears in the guise of the 'Lady of the Green Kirtle'— the Queen of the Underworld who transforms herself at the climax into a mammoth, crushing snake like a boa constrictor.

All of the threshold spirits make it into the book, in one way or another.

Forgetfulness is a repeated motif and the heroes are warned to be diligent and take practical steps to avoid it. Of course, they don't.

The spirit of wasting is represented by the thoughtlessly destructive giants of the wasteland. The army spirit is symbolised by the troops of mindlessly obedient gnomes; the vampire spirit by the owls;[61] the spirit of rejection by the increasing estrangement of Jill and Eustace. Only the spirit of backlash is represented by circumstances, rather than a specific character. It's seen in the collapse of the palace and surrounding city of the Underworld after the death of the Lady.

The main villain is, of course, the Lady-Python. She is clearly modelled on the sibyl of the Delphic Oracle—a priestess of ancient Greece who, possessed by a spirit of divination, was famed for her ambiguous predictions of the future. She was called 'the Pythoness', after Python Apollo, the tutelary deity worshipped at the shrine.

The book also details how we put ourselves into Python's hands through our own folly. It's true that the spirit misleads us through vague and confusing information. It's also true it silences those around us at critical moments. It's further true that the spirit tries to turn our decisions towards divination as we seek to navigate the 'if only' moments of life. However, regardless of all these subtle wiles of Python, we are ultimately responsible for the degree to which we allow ourselves to fall into its clutches as well as the level of our complicity with it.

But the story has the answer! As all the best happily-ever-afters do. As the children in the story call for help in the name of Aslan, the Great Lion, so we are to call for help in the name of Jesus, the Lion of the tribe of Judah. He is the only one who can show you how to defeat the threshold spirits, He is the only one who can safely open the threshold seals and He is the only all-sufficient sacrifice ever needed to pass safely into your calling.

'The heartstone of the problem is Nuada.'

Months and months of research enabled me to translate the sentence to 'The merlin of the problem is Merlin.'

And all that research, I decided at one point, was influencing my attempts to write a children's fantasy far too much. Long before I discovered threshold covenants, I started to have a suspicion that name covenants existed. I wouldn't have expressed it that way when I was stumbling through my first, awkward investigations. I simply said that lots of authors seemed to be struggling with their names. It didn't matter whether they were Christian or not.

CS 'Jack' Lewis, for instance, had written an entire series of books which featured a god-like lion named Aslan and which opened with a girl named Lucy finding her way through the back of a wardrobe into a land called Narnia where she met a faun under a lamp-post. Was it coincidental that Aslan meant *lion* in Turkish and *god of the land* in Old Norse and the surname Lewis was derived from the name of the Celtic god of light, *the lion of the steady hand*? Or that satyrs and fauns in English folklore were traditionally called Jack? I didn't think so.

Or, for a truly remarkable instance, consider the works of Toni

Morrison. I first read her books because I was looking for what the 'sul' of Sullivan meant and I had come to surmise it had a sense of *the falling sky*. Scratching around for evidence to corroborate or dismiss this theory, I noticed a book entitled *Sula*.

Now I had no idea Toni Morrison was a famous Afro-American winner of the Nobel Prize for Literature. I had no preconceptions about her work. But I knew Celtic imagery when I saw it. I knew some of the words uniquely associated with the Morrisons of the Isle of Lewis in the Outer Hebrides and there they were. When the eponymous title character of *Sula* killed Chicken Little, it seemed to fit my premise that 'sul' meant *the sky is falling*—as did the mysterious ending of *Song of Solomon*. Moreover, when the cold-hearted young woman in *Tar Baby* is described in a lustrous sealskin coat, I didn't think of black tar. I thought of lustrous sealskins. I thought of cold-hearted selkies. I thought of the folksong, *The Selkie of Sula Sgeir*.

And I wondered. Because by that time I knew Toni Morrison's background—that it wasn't Highland Scots and that Morrison was, in fact, her ex-husband's name. Could it be possible that the name she'd adopted was a greater influence on her identity and writing than her racial heritage?

There were also people like Philip Pullman, winner of the Whitbread Prize for the controversial children's fantasy, *The Amber Spyglass*.

This epic work is the finale to his trilogy, *His Dark Materials*. Profoundly anti-Christian in concept, it features God as an impotent, mad drooling sadist. Actually, perhaps it's unfair to label it anti-Christian, as that aspect is really only incidental. It is specifically and profoundly anti-CS Lewis.

Pullman wrote the trilogy after reading *The Chronicles of Narnia* and becoming incensed by Lewis' 'celebration of death' in *The Last Battle* and his abuse of the fantasy genre to promote Christian doctrine.

Personally I think this last criticism demonstrates Pullman's failure to understand what motivated Lewis. Not that he should be blamed for this. Lewis' own testimony that he simply started with an image that had been recurring in his mind's eye from the time he was a teenager—that of a faun standing with an umbrella near a snowy lamp-post—is not often believed by Christians either. Most people believe he set out to write dogma in allegorical form. If you're one of the readers who thinks this, ask yourself: if you were deliberately setting out to write Christian doctrine as a fairytale, would you start with a lion, a witch and a wardrobe? Wouldn't you choose something vastly more malleable to the theme?

Yes, we see images of roaring lions as Christ-figures everywhere on social media today—ubiquitous as never before in history—but only because Lewis pioneered the imagery. It's stayed the course as an image of a redeemer king in a way that, for example, John White's Gaal the Shepherd in the *Tower of Geburah* or Calvin Miller's King Ren in *The Chronicles of Singreale*, haven't. White seemed to be trying too hard to get across the symbolism of the classic tract, 'Four Spiritual Laws'. Miller, on the other hand, did seem to be less didactic. But I couldn't quite feel satisfied with his king, who had the habit of disappearing and transforming into a moondark creature which bloodily rended the kingdom's enemies limb from limb.

If, as has so often been stated over many decades, 'Christian writing' ultimately comes down to writing by Christians, I have a question. Why is the 'mind of Christ' so appealing in Narnia and Middle Earth but so disappointing in Singreale or Geburah?

It certainly isn't the skill of the author. White wrote the most exquisitely lyrical non-fiction but didn't seem able to bring it across to his fiction. And Calvin Miller's *The Singer* trilogy was an incomparable work of poetry. Pullman, likewise, is a superb writer, at least when he tones down the melodrama: anyone who can make me feel anguish over the severing of the tie between a daemon and a child, when my natural reaction would be to applaud the dismissal of a familiar spirit from its host, is a literary craftsman of the first water.

And frankly, I think that's what Pullman's opposition comes down to: the loathing of water for non-water.

It's about names, of course.

Philip Pullman's interpretation of God is no real bombshell once we realise that his first name means *lover of horses* and that horses are associated with the sea gods. For some bizarre reason, across many cultures, it was the sea gods who were considered the givers of horses to mankind. Poseidon in Greece, Neptune in Rome, Llyr in Celtic Britain.

From Shakespeare's time, Llyr was spelt 'Lear' and was associated with madness. In all the fuss about Pullman's work, a completely unremarked aspect is that, with a few exceptions, virtually all the adults are mad, bad and dangerous to know.

Certainly Lord Asriel and Mrs Coulter, the parents of the heroine Lyra Belacqua, are ambitious. However no one seems to have noted that their megalomania, coupled with their largely callous indifference to their child's existence, is exceedingly unnatural. The God-figure may be completely nuts in Pullman's universe, but those who would supplant him aren't backward in that regard either.

The whole story is, as far as I'm concerned, about Pullman's struggles with the dedication to the sea god, Llyr, hidden in his name. How much more obvious could it be when the heroine is Lyra Belacqua? Her first name is virtually the feminine of Llyr and her surname seems like Latin for *beautiful sea* or *beautiful water*.

The real reason, in my view, that Philip Pullman utterly loathed the work of CS Lewis is because Pullman takes on board Jungian acceptance of the daemon; an attitude Lewis turned his back on. His early pre-Christian poetry, written under the name Clive Hamilton, describes these spirits as finely as Pullman ever has. And amongst them is Nuada. Not unnaturally—Lewis was writing, after all, under the name 'Hamilton', his mother's maiden name.

The daemons are familiar spirits whose legal residence rights come from the dedication of the family name.

Are Pullman's daemons real? He suggested that he believes in them. I agree they are real; I disagree totally about what to do with them.

Pullman's ideas go back to Jung's description of the anima and animus. Jung, I was almost startled to find, was absolutely correct in his assessment of them—he wrote of the anima as a dark spirit inimical and utterly hostile to humanity. But then, incredibly, he turned around and called it by the Latin word for 'life' and suggested we embrace it.

I've read hundreds of authors and know what? This solution is instinctively avoided. I don't even think, at the end of the day, that Pullman wants to surrender in full allegiance to the daemons.

So, this is not just a Christian struggle, this 'power of the name' business and its attendant dedication. It is a struggle common to the human condition.

That's why you find Calvin Miller with a hero-king, Ren, whose alter-ego contains the word Grendel. And that's why Miller didn't quite manage to lick his story into line first-time: when the name within your name is the limb-rending monster from *Beowulf*, it might take a couple of goes to get it right. (And why on earth, you ask, would the name Miller have Grendel hidden in it? Because Grendel is from *grind*, and that's what mills and millers do.)

Lewis had several literary attempts at cleaning out the spiritually contamination of the 'lion of light' in his name before his eventual re-dedication of it to Christ in the *Narnia* series. He struggled for years until, like Jacob wrestling with God at the Ford of Jabbok, a new meaning was given to him. Through that new meaning that readers sense in *The Lion, the Witch and the Wardrobe*, countless people have been blessed.

Owen Barfield rightly says that 'when we can experience a change of meaning—a new meaning—there we may rightly join hands and sing with the morning stars; for there we are in at the birth. There is one of the exact points at which the genius, the *originality*, of the individual writer has first entered the world.'

When it comes to fiction, my belief is that Christian writing is that in which the power of the author's name is placed under the Lordship, and also in the service of, Christ. In practice this means that the 'mind of Christ' is not something like Athena's helmet which gifts us with automatic wisdom and insight and enables us to write perfectly about Christian doctrine or within a Christian worldview. It is something we have to work out, like our salvation, with fear and trembling; it is about the re-shaping of spiritual identity, the consequent re-forging of name; the choice to keep the power of that name in our own hands or place it in the wounded ones of the Lord of the Universe.

Of course not everyone is a writer.

So how do we expose the bedevilling spirits who hold guarantor status in our names and family lines? Two things, I believe, show them with great clarity.

First, the names themselves.

Secondly, our recurring dreams.

A friend had a repeating nightmare about her husband. In the dream, she would try to leave their house and he would wait in the doorway to kill her, a strange spade-like knife in his hand. Eventually she would always leave the house safely by the window.

Not unnaturally she was very disturbed by this dream. However when it became apparent that her husband never left his post by the door, it was then clear the nightmare was more about threshold guardians than about any genuine homicidal tendencies of her husband. The unusual aspect of the dream symbolism was therefore not his hostility but the strange knife. What did that signify?

Starting with her husband's name it didn't take too long to find what name covenant was involved. Tyler is from *tiler* and, like tailor, it derives its original meaning from *one who cuts*. This explained the strange spade-like knife: it was a tiling tool. But why was a tiler associated with a threshold guardian?

That also didn't take too long to discover, either. The 'tyler' of the Masonic tradition was charged with guarding the doorways, sword drawn, to kill any person, Mason or not, who might have nefarious intent towards the Lodge.

Going back to Philip Pullman, we find a similar sort of threshold guardian exposed in his stories. The Roman god equivalent to the Celtic Llyr is the one in charge of gates, doorways, bridges, first things, the New Year.[62] Janus, after whom January is named, was a deity with two faces: one facing forward and one backward. As Januspater, *Father Janus*, he was the most ancient of the Latin gods.

No doubt Sigmund Freud would have attributed the obvious desire in Pullman's trilogy to kill the father, and Father God most of all, to an Oedipus complex. Personally however I suspect the daemon Januspater simply wants to kill any father it sees as a usurper. Just as I suspect Freud's own obsession with Eros and Thanatos, *sex* and *death*, goes back to the derivation of his name from Frey, the Norse god of sex, and his sister Freyja, the goddess of love, who claimed half the dead from war god Odin.

Despite Freud's beliefs about the universality of the desire to kill the father and marry the mother, I believe such wishes are name-specific.

Similarly, the fear that 'the man I call my father is not really my father' tends to correlate very strongly with particular names—most especially in families named Morrison. Such an unfounded fear is not about present circumstances but rather the mythic foundations of the name. According to Robert Graves, the name 'Morrison' is derived from the practice of Morris dancing. Originally part of the festivities associated with a fertility rite, Morris dancers were probably named for the blackening of their faces. This disguise was sometimes augmented by the wearing of animal skins or masks, making the dancers seem part-human, part-animal: like fauns or satyrs.

At the culmination of the dance, one of the performers—selected by lot—would be ceremonially sacrificed; beheaded. The 'robin' was killed by the 'jack'.

The night before this happened, however, there was a ritualistic orgy. Naturally nine months later, quite a few children would be born. If the mother knew the identity of the father, she'd call the child

Robinson or Jackson—*son of the robin* or *son of the jack*. But if she didn't know his identity, she would just plump for the more generic name, Morrison, *son of a Morris dancer*.

If she later wed, it was very much the case that the child conceived during the festivities could grow up, not knowing for a considerable time that his dad was not in fact his biological father.

Twenty, forty, maybe sixty generations on, the origin of Morrison can still spiritually impact those who bear the name. Why does it go on so long? After all, God promises us that a curse will influence, at most, three or four generations.

The issue is that this is not actually a curse in its own right.

It's a name covenant. And a covenant has no end-date, no termination clause, no let-out condition.

We have to go before the Judgment Seat of God, revoke our agreement with the covenant undertaken by our ancestors and ask for it to be made null and void. This may sound simple—but there may also be threshold covenants involved. We have to ask God to do what He did for Jesus at His resurrection: scare off the guard, remove the stone, break open the seals.

Specifically, individually and personally.

Because the breaking of a seal is so dangerous, it's worth pausing here, for a moment, to ask for God's shielding. *Father God, I pray for Your protective kiss over anyone reading this section.*

Not long after I had translated 'the heartstone of the problem is Nuada' to 'the merlin of the problem is Merlin', the children's fantasy I was writing started to have vague allusions to Merlin. At the time, I was deliberately writing to see if Jung's assertion was true that the subconscious actively tries to conceal the messages of the unconscious from the conscious. Or whether, if I deliberately pushed the symbolism in my writing as far as possible without distorting it, I'd discover something about my name I didn't know before.

The main symbols in the fantasy were trees, hands, time, forgiveness, twins, giant giraffe-like horses. These giants seemed to be the mythic element—they were, without any doubt, based on the giants of *The Silver Chair* who were in turn based on the ettins of Anglo-Saxon myth and were related to the ents of Tolkien's *The Lord of The Rings*.

Why I picked those giants I had no idea. I didn't find them an attractive element of *The Silver Chair* at all. I wondered why Lewis included them in the book until I realised it starts out with mythic overtones from the nursery rhyme, *Jack and Jill*, reminiscent of Lewis' nickname, Jack, before turning to elements of *Jack and the Beanstalk*.

In *On Stories*, he writes that something in nature compels us to invent giants. And only giants, he says, will do to describe these wild, atmospheric emanations that riddle us with fear and awe. He goes on to wonder if it is coincidence that Wordsworth heard heavy breathings in the fells of North England, in the same kind of landscape where the hero of the medieval poem, *Sir Gawain and the Green Knight*, found 'etins aneleden him'— *giants came blowing after him*.

When I first read *On Stories*, these three ancient words 'etins aneleden him' detonated with such force, I thought the connection between my spirit and body had been shattered by some sort of explosive decompression. My whole being felt as if it had been blasted apart and parts were soaring, out of control, into the stratosphere.

Coherent thought was impossible for hours and, when it was, all I could think was: 'How can three words do that? Why didn't they do it when I was reading *Sir Gawain and the Green Knight* for myself?'

Because they're not there, that's why. Lewis was obviously quoting from memory and, while the concept does appear, these exact words don't.

God's mercy is great. I'd touched a seal and felt the nuclear blast in my spirit but He had shielded me tremendously. Seals are designed to inflict huge damage, even to kill.

Is there, as Lewis says, something in nature that compels us to invent giants?

I think that, like Freud with his theories of Eros and Thanatos, like the Morrisons with their concerns about their fathers, Lewis couldn't imagine that his need to invent giants was a name-specific concern and not a universal human fixation.

Lewis wrote his early poetry under the pseudonym, 'Clive Hamilton'. Hamilton therefore became a name he had to deal with. In *The Silver Chair* and, more particularly, *The Last Battle*, he attempts to resolve the dedication of the name 'Hamilton'.

He also looks to his own hopes for his life's calling. Lewis didn't want to be known as a novelist nearly as much as he wanted to be a famous poet. His heart's desire for many years was to be like the bard who won the eisteddfod for his skill at poetry and was awarded the 'silver chair'. But, as he must have realised, his desire was tainted by a temptation he battled for many years: a drawing towards the occult.

That too was in the names he was born with and chose to assume.

When I finished my book about thirteen trees, wounded hands, time running backwards, forgiveness, twins and giant green giraffe-like horses, I wondered if I could really call it *Merlin's Wood* when it didn't actually have Merlin in it. Just echoes of Merlin. Would readers be disappointed? Would they feel cheated?

I took the risk and did it anyway.

It seemed to me, for quite some time, that Jung was right. The subconscious must filter messages from the unconscious so they are never received by the conscious mind. Because, despite all my efforts to tap into the deeps of my name, I could see absolutely nothing of 'Hamilton' in the story. I knew what the symbols of the name were and, despite my deliberate attempts to include them, the story had gone elsewhere. My experiment was a failure.

But I was left with a question: what exactly were the puzzling symbols in my story all about?

It didn't take long to uncover a connection. The majority of them came from an ancient Welsh poem called *The Battle of the Trees*. That didn't make any sense. I wasn't Welsh. As for the appearance of Merlin's Wood but not Merlin, I couldn't make out any reason whatsoever.

Then one day, about a year later, my mum asked me a question that caused me to research the family name from a different angle. I discovered that Hamilton hadn't necessarily always been the name of my ancestors. Some present day Hamiltons were originally named Cadzow.

Cadzow is a Scottish locality, first recorded in the sixth century. The Queen of Cadzow is mentioned and appears to be, through matching legend and history, the twin sister of the wild man who came to be known in later ages as Merlin. Cadzow was part of the old Caledonian forest, the section around the present-day town of Hamilton. It was indeed 'Merlin's Wood'.

Cadzow has many possible translations, but the one that immediately leapt out at me is *battle of the ettins*, that is, *battle of the trees*.

It took me a long while to realise how wrong Jung was.

Our subconscious doesn't try to repress or suppress our story. Our dreams aren't filtered to try to keep our shameful, unconscious desires in check. The symbolism that baffles us isn't a desperate shift to keep us from the experience of gnawing guilt, self-hatred or self-reproach.

The symbolism of recurring dreams is a divine translation, with corroborating elements, revealing the spiritual guarantor who holds the legal rights to our names. God is not slow to let us know what our problem is. We are simply slow to understand.

And slower still to ask for His help.

It is idle, having planted an acorn in the morning, to expect that afternoon to sit in the shade of the oak.

Antoine de Saint-Exupéry, *Wind, Sand and Stars*

Shing had been a threshold sacrifice for her fiancé. After forging her name on some company documents, he had defrauded investors of millions of dollars, leaving her to face a prison sentence. As Shing began to rebuild her life, she recognised that every time God extended His hand to draw her into her calling, a crushing blow would fall.

Then she learned of the existence of threshold covenants and name covenants.

In China, the knowledge of threshold guardians and the power of names has almost faded but has not vanished so completely as in the West. She quickly grasped the relationship between threshold and name; and took all the preliminary steps towards evicting Python, Rachab and Leviathan from her life.

She repented of her false refuge. She waited for the subsequent test and passed it—heading straight for God when she was next disappointed.

She renounced the covenant with death over her family line; and she prayed for Jesus to purify her name. After several days, she rang me—worried. 'Nothing has happened,' she said. Shing had been influenced too much by Western Christianity with its expectations of instant results: while she didn't have an oak-from-an-acorn-in-a-day mentality, she still thought signs of something happening should appear after nearly a week.

'We've planted a seed,' I told her. 'Don't dig it up every few days to see how it's going.'

Months later, however, she was seriously worried. The 'unnatural natural' event that God promises in Isaiah 28:21 as a sign He has swept away the covenant with death was not forthcoming. My reassurances that God works across seasons, growing and maturing faith within us, weren't fully allaying her increasing doubts.

Then the breakthrough came! And, on a count back to the day of renunciation of the covenant with death, we found it was the same specific number of days I have normally observed when anyone renounces this covenant. I'm not going to say what that number is because I don't want to put God in a box—or anyone's expectations of Him either.

Shing was ready to ask God for His permission to place the cherubim onto her threshold. She prayed again about her name and we asked God, in His mercy, to send a pair of cherubim to chase away the threshold guardians and also to reveal the seals over her name as well as the inscription on her threshold stone.

Many months passed. 'People don't realise how long this takes,' Shing said whenever she'd hear people talk about threshold covenants.

'There's a reason why God says the cornerstone in Zion has engraved on it, *Those who believe will not be in haste*,' I said.

One day hell broke loose. It was a 'threshold' day, of course—when many new things were being implemented.

On a single day, Shing was involved in a major car accident; her fledgling new enterprise was threatened with devastating losses; members of her family threw unjust accusations at her and walked out of her life.

She rang, in tears and perplexity. 'This shouldn't be happening! If I have passed over the threshold and God is my covenant defender, why am I still being sacrificed?'

'I will pray for you,' I told her. 'But two things come to mind: first, that other people will always be trying to cross their own thresholds and that you may find yourself on their testing ground. The risk that they will try to sacrifice you will always be there, but with God as your covenant defender, your response will be different. You won't be tempted to sacrifice yourself or them. At least you shouldn't be.' I paused. 'However, God may not yet be your covenant defender. I want you to go away and ask Him what all these troubles are about.'

Shing rang back the next day. 'You'll never guess! God said to me: "*You have other gods before Me.*" And I said, "*What?!*" And He reminded me of something that happened when I was four years old. I'd forgotten all about it. My auntie was baby-sitting me and had taken me with her when she visited a friend. They put me in a back room with some toys while they chatted to each other. Soon I was scared but no one came to get me. A long time went by and I became more and more fearful they had forgotten about me. Then I saw a statue, high on a wall. I don't know how, but suddenly I knew its name. And I asked it to rescue me. I prayed to it, pleaded with it.'

'And soon your aunt came?'

'Yes. I was so happy. But, you know, I haven't thought about what happened from that day until God brought it up yesterday. Is that all it takes to worship another god?'

Shing had already repented of her action but we took the time to sever any lingering ties with the demon she'd encountered. Her story is not an unusual one—for many of us, small forgotten traumas are hidden in the mists of childhood. Moments when we were vulnerable and reacted in ways that served the purposes of hell rather than the advancement of heaven. Moments that have long slid away into the far recesses of remembrance, not because the memory was repressed or suppressed but because, in the end, our hearts were comforted.

Just like Shing's aunt arriving at a critical moment, someone came to help us and, relieved at the outcome, we put the incident behind us.

'Isn't it all done at the Cross?' I hear some people ask.

The Cross is the supply for all we need to apply.

It isn't a magic talisman, a one-time-cure-all pill or an automatic sanctification dispenser—it's the means by which we begin covenant with Jesus and, through Him, the Father.

From it comes the empowering grace to do the impossible: to remain faithful and so be invited to cut other covenants; to pass awkward tests; to mend history.

Mick was not only sexually molested as a child but subjected to satanic ritual abuse. At just four years old, he was forced to participate in harrowing black masses in order to save his little sister's life. Naturally he suffered from dissociative identity disorder.

Mick came to see my mother and me about a covenant with death. We dealt with some generational issues and, although we had no expertise with satanic ritual abuse—he decided he'd like to continue prayer ministry with us anyway.

The good thing about dissociative identity disorder is the rapid, discordant shifts of subject associated with it. Mick constantly apologised for letting his mind wander down rabbit trails, leaving some parts of his story unfinished while picking up the scent of another vaguely related episode. But, as I said, a good thing.

One day, Mick started out a conversation that jumped from one odd thought to the next: Pleiades, anchor and John the Baptist.

They sounded suspiciously like seals to me.

I started collecting the 'nonsense' words as Mick recalled his early life and tried to articulate the vows surrounding his experience of satanic abuse. Amongst half a dozen others was an immensely powerful vow governing all the rest: 'I don't want to do anything that will trigger the programming.'

Mick sensed his hidden programming involved murder and incest.

I couldn't think of any way to safely revoke or renounce a vow like that. Yet none of the other vows would fall unless this 'governor' did. And its existence explained why all of the counselling and therapy Mick had received over the years was, at best, marginally effective. Repenting and renouncing might trigger his programming, so although he'd been through the motions, it wasn't with all his heart.

Then it occurred to me. If what triggered the programming could be removed, then the vow could be dismantled—and that would pave the way to dismantling the entire structure.

All that was necessary was to find the number of seals and their nature. Their nature should reveal the identity of the ruling spirit. But Pleiades, anchor and John the Baptist didn't make sense. At least they did make sense in one way, but not in the most important one. They were all related to water: but Mick's name was from Michael which has no water aspect at all.

Michael is the angelic prince of covenant Israel and means '*who is like the Lord?*' The name encodes the tension between covenant and contract—between oneness and likeness. There's no hint of water in it anywhere.

I asked Mick if he remembered a satanic baptism. He had a sudden memory flash and thought there was a strong possibility that was the case. Such a baptism involves actual drowning, followed by resuscitation. Because such a baptism is a counterfeit of church infant baptism, then it involves a name and a dedication to a god. Basically it's a name covenant with a demon.

Of course, most name covenants *are* just that; otherwise we wouldn't see the likes of CS Lewis, John White, Calvin Miller, Toni Morrison and Philip Pullman wrestling with the myth encoded in their names.

A short chat to the Holy Spirit and we quickly uncovered seven seals. Unbelievable. Incredible. It was staggeringly easy. I was used to spending months consulting the Holy Spirit, cautiously collecting information so that there was no possibility of the removal of one seal triggering the others or any hidden programming kicking in. It was startling to have everything come out in half an hour. I found out later that Mick had spent many months inviting the Lord into the whole of his being daily—and that undoubtedly accounted for the speed of the revelation.

He happened to mention in the course of uncovering these seven water-related seals that he'd long had a desire to go canoeing on a lake. However he was unable to do so because he was afraid of being drowned. He felt an inordinate fear a water spirit would get him.

That was enough of a clue. There was a name, very like Mick, that was derived from 'water spirit'. It was Nick.

The Satan's most skilful work is the infinitesimal twist, the subtle misdirection, the tiny but diabolic misalignment. Nick can derive from 'neck', 'nicor' or 'nixie', the water spirits of Germanic mythology.

Normally in dealing with a name covenant, there is an aspect of restoring the true name. But not in this case. We asked Jesus to uncover the demonic seals, open the false scroll and tear it up, remove all copies of the record in it from heaven, hell and earth.

That done, Mick was able to renounce his governing vow, as well as half a dozen other significant vows.

As we finished, he testified to a surprising outcome. His sense of dissociation had almost completely vanished. At first, I thought it was God's sweet bonus—because we hadn't prayed about that aspect at all.

Then I realised.

Identity comes from name.

Dissociative identity disorder: could it simply be a *name* disorder?

Could it be about a demonic superstructure involving a false name covenant?

I'm still researching this possibility. However I am convinced this could well be God's breakthrough blessing for some people who have suffered all their lives from the after-effects of ritual abuse.

5

The Bridegroom of Blood

WHAT DOES A DEFILED THRESHOLD look like? It's one where blessing is constantly siphoned off, where divine promises seem to about to finally come to fruition only to crumble to dust before your eyes, where constriction, wasting and backlash are so consistent and severe, there seems to be no let-up, no breathing space.

On a defiled threshold, we are disappointed over and over. And if we don't give up, we'll build up a litany of excuses to explain our lack of breakthrough:

- 'I guess I didn't hear God's voice, after all.' (Despite the promise of Jesus that His sheep hear His voice.)
- 'Maybe I didn't have enough faith.' (But we only need a mustard seed's worth.)
- 'I shouldn't have listened to the doubters.' (As if positive thoughts determine the breakthrough, and not Jesus.)
- 'It can't have been God's will.' (As if God's will is always done on earth as it is in heaven! Why would we be asked to pray for it if it were a foregone conclusion?)
- 'It seems God is teaching me patience.'

Years after God has taught some of us astronomical levels of patience, we can find ourselves stuck in the rut of this excuse. 'I guess I'll just have to wait on God,' we say as we stop trying. In doing so, we put ourselves into the hands of the spirit of wasting: Rachab 'the do-nothing'.

We allow ourselves to become idle, thinking we're 'waiting'. We vigilantly hold our hopes under because letting them surface is too heart-breaking. Soon we're no longer ready if opportunity arrives. We fail to invest in ongoing preparation for our calling. We become depressed.

It's not good enough to revoke our agreements with Python if those with Rachab still exist.

It's simply, as the cliché goes, 'out of the frying pan into the fire.'

Of all the tragedies Scripture recounts, few are more heart-rending than the story of Jephthah and his daughter.

It goes like this: Jephthah is a mighty man of valour who makes a rash vow. He promises God that, if heaven gives him victory over the Ammonites, then whatever he first encounters on crossing the threshold to his house on his return will be sacrificed to the Lord. He wins the battle and, as he returns home in triumph, his daughter rushes out to welcome him.

As the story progresses to its disturbing ending, the moral seems to be: don't make rash vows. But a little digging suggests a lesson a little more subtle.

The meaning of the name Jephthah is usually given as *opening* with the implication of *Yahweh will open*. However the name is related to 'miphtan', *defiled threshold*, and derives from 'pethen', *python*. Thus it has overtones that are nowhere near as innocuous as the sanitised rendering, *Yahweh will open*, suggests.

Just as Elijah means *El is Yahweh*, then it may well be that Jephthah means *Python is Yahweh*. When your name means that *the twisting, constricting guardian of the threshold is the supreme God*, it's no wonder that, despite your best intentions, your vows are (1) related to threshold matters and (2) perverted.

In my view, the real moral of the story is: if yours is a defiled threshold—indicated by the continual constriction and wasting you experience—then it's wise to take counsel with others when any vows whatsoever are undertaken. This super-caution regarding promises to God or to men is required because the spirit of Python will twist your vow. You will be forced to choose between sin and sin: between breaking your word and doing something both you and God abhor. Either way your integrity is sacrificed. Either way you dishonour God. Either way you lose big time.

Jephthah's story is not the only one in Scripture to caution us about threshold covenants. Almost every hero story in the Book of Judges recalls an episode of threshold covenant violation and then goes on to recount the consequences of such abuse. The theme of this set of stories is in my opinion very clear: as Paul says in Galatians 6:7, we reap what we sow. If we abuse a threshold covenant, then we can expect to have the same happen to us. We are not above justice but are judged with the same measure as that we mete out to others.

The very name—book of Judges—is apt. The judges of the ancient world sat in the gateways: they are therefore threshold guardians. Hence the stories about threshold covenant in this section of Scripture are completely fitting in nature. The repeated refrain that, during this period of history, everyone did 'what was right in his own eyes' assures us that we are reading about those who judged themselves—and did not find their own actions reprehensible.

Although the episodes are mostly in chronological order, the last few seem to be well out of time sequence and probably occurred earlier in the period of the Judges rather than later. The writer seems to have chosen an ordering where the gravity of threshold offence escalates as the stories progress. In the first few stories, threshold violation is either comparatively minor or can be considered a sin of the enemy. But, gradually a shift occurs. This is a work with a literary twist. Once it's established just how despicable the enemy Philistines are, the sting is in operation. If the reader has judged the Philistines for their covenant violation, the far worse behaviour of the Israelites will come across with much more impact.

The story cycle starts with Othniel, a nephew of Caleb, who defeated a king of Mesopotamia and gave the land peace for forty years. Fine detail is lacking in this opening report, making it a stark contrast to the next half-comic tale about Ehud, a left-handed warrior of the tribe of Benjamin.[63]

Threshold markers are scattered across Ehud's story but they don't seem to carry much weight of disapproval with them.

A party of ambassadors is sent with tribute to Eglon, the king of Moab, who had the Israelites under his very considerable fat thumb. When the ambassadors return home, Ehud goes with them as far as Gilgal. He then re-crosses the Jordan, returning to Moab alone. He asks to speak privately to the king. The doors are closed and the message Ehud delivers is a knife to the gut. Escaping, he blows the trumpet to call Ephraim to war. He then leads the troops to the ford of the Jordan where they kill ten thousand Moabites, allowing none to 'pass over'.

The story's threshold markers are the mention of the doors, Gilgal at the fords of the Jordan and the comment that none were allowed to 'pass over'. There seems no point in bringing Gilgal to the reader's attention except that it's where the Israelites under Joshua had camped after 'passing over' the Jordan. A threshold location, it was where the people had been circumcised to show their ratification of the covenant. It was also where Joshua cut the covenant with the Gibeonites.

Whether Ehud violated a threshold covenant when he killed the king is unclear. The reiteration that the slaying occurred in a roof chamber may be meant to assure the reader that Ehud had technically kept the letter, if not the spirit, of the custom. Still it seems to be an ambiguous case and perhaps that was even the view of the writer of Judges. So it's an appropriate story to begin with, if the writer's plan was to present the reader with ever more serious situations of offence.

After a single verse about Shamgar who killed several hundred Philistines with an oxgoad, there's the extended story of Deborah. Here the first of the unambiguous threshold covenant violations is recounted.

It occurs when the enemy commander Sisera is fleeing from the armies of Barak and Deborah. He comes to the tents of Heber the Kenite and is greeted by Heber's wife, Jael. Inviting him into the tent, she agrees to hide him from all pursuit. The moment he accepts and steps over the threshold, a covenant comes into play between the host and the guest: Jael is required to defend him to the death and he is likewise required to defend her. Sisera asks her to stand at the threshold, while he hides under coverings. Jael agrees to lie about his whereabouts, if necessary.[64] She simply at this point confirms the covenant she's already made with him. She behaves just as Rahab did in an earlier age when, because of a threshold covenant with two spies, she lied to protect their lives.

Jael offers Sisera milk—a further indication of how seriously she took the covenant. A skin of milk in ancient times could only be preserved with salt—thus she went beyond threshold covenant to salt covenant. She ratifies her covenant with Sisera at least four times.

So when he falls asleep and Jael kills him, an ancient reader would have been vastly more shocked than we moderns are. She committed a barbaric crime[65] and was praised for breaching covenant!

This is stylistic storytelling at its very best: to surprise the reader with a completely unexpected, shocking series of events and to stack up the mystery. The writer has held back a crucial piece of information—a literary technique he will use again, to even greater effect.

So what is the hidden detail that changes the whole scenario? It's that Sisera was killed inside *her* tent—that is, within the women's section of the tent.

Bishop KC Pillai explained the significance of this: the women's section is at the heart of a tent, divided from the men's section by a curtain. In modern times, not even police can enter this space. Wars, he insisted in *Light Through An Eastern Window*, have been fought over the issue.

Now the pursuers of Sisera would be excessively unlikely to insult

Jael as she stood at the door of the tent and ask to search the men's quarters. Even if they did, it would be absolutely unthinkable for them to consider entering the women's section. An inviolable sanctum, this is a place Sisera should never have entered. By doing so, he proclaimed Jael's covenantal vows worthless. He didn't trust her as a covenant defender—either because he thought she was lying or because he thought she'd waver under pressure.

His action was a betrayal that put *her* life on the line. An honour killing was the almost inevitable outcome. If anyone ever found he'd been there, Jael's virtue and reputation would have been destroyed and she herself would have been put to death to preserve the standing of her relatives in the tribe.

At the moment she finds Sisera inside her part of the tent, her options become severely limited. To kill or to die.

She chooses to save her own life and kill Sisera.

Here we have another moral related to threshold covenant: don't deliberately put your host's life in mortal danger. If you do, you violate the covenant and therefore the situation is no longer as black and white as it once was, should your host react by ignoring the covenant as well.

The dilemma Jael faced is not as uncommon as it might seem. Many of us face a similar choice regularly when it comes to threshold issues: do we sacrifice ourselves or the person who has betrayed us? Do we sacrifice the honour of our heavenly Father or do we really and truly believe that Jesus is the all-sufficient sacrifice to save us in whatever horrific circumstances we find ourselves?

Because our choices are generally more subtle than Jael's—far less clear-cut in circumstance or consequence—our sacrifices tend to be unnoticed, even to ourselves. They're fenced with rationalisation and justification.

And unlike Jael, we don't know threshold covenant violation when we see it. We can't recognise it—either in ourselves or others. We are generally ignorant of the symptoms that show its presence in ourselves or our family line.

Even if we do notice them, then sometimes—like Gideon, at the beginning of the next story in the sequence—we don't want to rock the boat.

The appearance of a pair of angels is a sure indication of a threshold event. Even one should be enough to suggest we look more closely. At the beginning of Gideon's story, he's threshing wheat in a winepress—hiding from marauding Midianites.

An angel appears with the greeting: 'The Lord is with you, mighty man of valour.' Gideon is taken aback and asks a few questions. Then, despite his doubts, he duplicates at the oak of Ophrah the same sort of hospitality as Abraham had offered long before at the oaks of Mamre.

Just as Abraham prepared a meal and partook of a threshold covenant with God and His angels, so Gideon acted in a similar fashion. He killed a goat and prepared a broth to pour out on an altar. Now every threshold stone is an altar—the original 'kaph', *cornerstone*, eventually becoming the 'kapporeth', *mercy-seat*, of the Ark of the Covenant. So, Gideon covenanted with God through this sacrifice.

In a flash, the angel consumed the sacrifice and disappeared. Gideon was scared and stunned. However, he was also convinced.

For a moment he was sure he was going to die. But when he was reassured, he gave God a name: *the Lord is peace.*

That night God impressed on him the need to be single-minded in his devotion. So, despite being afraid of the repercussions, Gideon went out under cover of darkness and cut down an altar to Baal. Despite the hostility of the town, he won a new name for his exploits: 'Jerub-baal', *let Baal contend with him.*

Angel, sacrifice, hospitality: threshold markers that show it was all about Gideon, a timid man, pushing past his fears to relate to God in a new way—as covenant defender. Since threshold covenants made with God are also associated with name covenants, it is no surprise that there is a name exchange in operation here. Gideon gives God a name, *the Lord is peace*.

Prior to this, however, the angel hails Gideon, *hewer*, as a 'mighty man of valour', using a word, *valour*, that also means *army*. The first syllable of Gideon's name has that same meaning: *troop* or *army*. So God redefined the name of the *hewer* to tell him he was called to lead armies, not just chop down things.

Like Gideon, Moses was a timid man who would much have preferred God to choose someone else as the deliverer of His people. Confronted by an angel in a burning bush, Moses expressed considerable doubt he'd be able to perform the task, even with God's help.

Now while Gideon allowed himself to be convinced by some unnatural events involving dew and a woollen fleece, Moses refused to be convinced even when God demonstrated His power with two signs: first, a staff turning into a snake, and second, a hand turning leprous.

Moses resisted God's call. And he continued to resist and reject it—so much so, that a few days after this encounter on Mount Sinai, God tried to kill him!

It's difficult to be certain but subtle hints about this encounter at Sinai suggest God was offering Moses a name covenant. In such a covenant, names are revealed and exchanged: for example, God reveals Himself to Abram as El Shaddai and then offers him a new name 'Abraham', giving him the fruitful 'h' of His own name.

Here with Moses, God reveals an entirely new name, Ehyeh—and, no, I haven't spelled Yahweh wrongly here. Yahweh is a step removed from the sacred name, Ehyeh, and means *He is who he is*. Ehyeh means *I am who I am*.

Does God offer Moses a new name? With as subtle a change as that of Abram to Abraham?

I believe so. Just prior to God's first attempt to convince Moses to accept the call, He asks, 'What is it in your hand?'

'What is it' is from 'mazeh'—a rhyme with 'moseh', *Moses*.

The 'it' God referred to—Moses' staff—turns into a snake. This symbol of the Pharaohs was integral to the double crown of Egypt with its frontal cobra ready to strike.

The symbolism is unmistakeable: God has crafted the perfect deliverer in Moses—the shepherd's staff says he knows how to care for a wandering, recalcitrant flock; the snake says he can navigate the court customs of the Egyptian royal house. In addition, he is fluent in several languages, has decades of wilderness survival skills, and a burning sense of justice that will enable a codification of law to be passionately conveyed to a stiff-necked people.

Moses at this point is himself as stiff-necked as the people God was sending him to. We can be sure of this because, just a few days later, God tried to kill him over a threshold covenant. Moses, with an incredible call on his life, with God sparing no effort to reassure him either with miraculous signs or emotional support through his brother, turns his back on it all. His defiance when it came to God's call was to have huge repercussions throughout the history of Israel.

When Moses entered the 'inn' in the desert, he covenanted with the host—just as the two spies who entered Jericho some forty years after this did with Rahab. A threshold covenant was as simple as passing over a cornerstone and eating with the host. Through this action the guest and the host come into oneness—thus it is apparent by God's attempt to kill Moses that he was no longer one with God, if ever he had been. He had treacherously[66] chosen instead to seek protection with some other person or god totally opposed to the Holy One of the Burning Bush.

God repudiates all covenantal defence of Moses and turns on him. Zipporah re-confirms the covenant through a sudden swift circumcision and saves Moses' life. All this is by way of illustrating how seriously God takes threshold covenant.

And how, if He offers you a new name, it's wise to use Gideon as your role model and not Moses.

All goes well with Gideon for some time. He becomes the leader of an army, which God soon whittles down to three hundred—and those brave few follow him as he uses a stratagem to alarm the Midianites and set them to fighting each other.

After an extended, wide-ranging battle, the Midianites are defeated and the Israelites ask Gideon, whom they have also come to call 'Jerubbaal',[67] to rule over them. He wisely refused—but unwisely took some of the plunder and made an ephod out of the gold. This breastplate of a high priest came to be a spiritual snare to Gideon and his family since all of Israel came to worship it. His certainly wasn't the only family for whom an ephod was a snare: it was also to prove a temptation down the line for the family of Moses.

After Gideon, the next judge of Israel who had any major story cycle told about him was Jephthah. However, prior to Jephthah's elevation as a judge, the covenant between God and His people breaks down entirely.

A king was appointed in Israel. Not over all Israel, as would happen later with Saul, but over a significant section of the tribal alliance. Now, Israel had covenanted with God that the people would have no king but Him alone. When Gideon's son, Abimelech, decided he wanted the kingship his father had refused, his defiance of God became blatant. After killing all but one of his seventy brothers on a single stone in Orphah, he was acclaimed as king under an oak in one of the cities of refuge: Shechem.

Abimelech has, like many Hebrew names, more than one meaning: *desired counsel* and *my father is king*. Since Gideon had refused the kingship offered to him, we can be reasonably sure that he meant his son's calling to be that of a wise counsellor whose advice was eagerly sought.[68] Names always encode a choice, however, and Abimelech seems that have decided his father's decision to forfeit the kingship was an error.

So to come into the calling he has determined he will gain for himself, he analyses the situation and sees the obvious threshold sacrifice needed to ensure his destiny as the first king of Israel. His seventy brothers. The fact he slays almost all of them on the same stone suggests a deliberate blood offering. Only Jotham escapes the threshold sacrifice.

Abimelech is not simply a man of cruelty and ruthless ambition: his rebellion against God is calculated, arrogant and perverse.

The proclamation of his kingship took place in a location designed to provoke maximum offence to heaven: this oak tree in Shechem was a hallowed spot from earliest times. It was where Abram built the first of seven altars to God in the Promised Land; where Jacob buried the idols of his former life and reaffirmed his covenant with God; where Joshua, at the end of his life, called on the stone pillar there to be a witness as the people reaffirmed their covenant with God. It was close by Jacob's Well and Joseph's tomb—and those of the other patriarchs as well.

It lay between the mountains Ebal and Gerizim which formed a natural amphitheatre where sound was magnified. Even before they entered the Promised Land, Moses told the people they were to go to these heights, having split into two tribal groupings, and there proclaim covenantal curses and blessings at each other. They had obeyed that command. Their words would have echoed down to the valley and reverberated to this very spot where Abimelech chose to be crowned.

The oak tree with its stone pillar was a place designated to retain the memory of ancient covenants and also to be a memorial to them; the landscape itself was a witness to events recorded in stone and tree.

In a later age, Jesus would sit somewhere here, probably at this very spot, to speak to the first person to suggest that He was the Messiah: the woman of Samaria who became his first evangelist.

Abimelech not only broke covenant with God but lured the people of Shechem into doing the same. As a city of refuge, they were charged with additional responsibility and authority. Shechem, meaning *shoulder* or *saddle*, has both a connotation of government and mandated authority. In Hebrew culture, when a man passed his authority to another, he would do so by laying keys upon the other person's shoulder. Hence the famous phrase in Isaiah 9:6 that '*the government shall be upon His shoulder*' simply refers to the possession of keys with heavenly and earthly authority.

The people of Shechem, in agreeing to Abimelech's proposal and giving him money to hire mercenaries to help him slaughter his brothers, abrogated the very responsibility that was the calling of their town elders.

Jotham, Abimelech's sole surviving brother, made sure the people knew the spiritual implications of crowning his bloodthirsty sibling. Climbing Mount Gerizim, he shouted down to the valley, knowing that he would be heard. The words of his opening, '*If you have acted in good faith and honour when you made Abimelech king…*' used identical phrasing to that of Joshua's charge to the people to be faithful to God's covenant in the same spot.[69]

Making covenant. Breaking covenant. Abimelech seems to have orchestrated his move against God's covenant, ensuring it occurred at the same place where so often previously the covenant had been ratified, reaffirmed and renewed.

It should therefore be no surprise to us to realise Abimelech was killed by a stone.

He defiled a stone, sacrificed his brothers on it, defied God—and the natural result of reaping what he'd sown was a bigger stone with crippling consequences. A few years later, during a siege, a woman threw a millstone down on him.

Sometimes our lives are entangled with covenant-breakers like Abimelech. The worst choice when we find that is the case is to abdicate authority and responsibility as the people of Shechem did.

The Glory was entrusted to you, you weren't given permission to pass it on as you see fit.

Michael Ende, The Neverending Story

After the salutary lesson of Abimelech and its obvious moral, the book of Judges moves on to Jephthah. We've already seen this is another story with yet another moral about defiled threshold covenants.

So too is the next episode about a person of any significance: Samson.

The famous interlude with Delilah is testimony to the adage we've already noted in the story of Abimelech: you reap what you sow. Not only that, you reap the same kind of 'crop' as the seed you sowed. To see Samson as an exemplar of this principle, note that, before getting involved with Delilah, Samson had visited the town of Gaza and hooked up with a prostitute.

At this point in his career, he'd already made himself exceedingly unpopular with the Philistine overlords by killing a thousand of them with a donkey's jawbone. So when they realised he was in town, they decided to wait by the city gates until morning and kill him as he departed.

However, Samson decided to leave at midnight and, realising some would-be assassins were waiting for him, he uprooted the town gates, put them on his shoulders and carried them until he reached the hill overlooking Hebron. Is this bizarre behaviour or *super*-bizarre behaviour? Are we truly expected to believe that the Philistines couldn't achieve their goal, despite losing the element of surprise, when Samson is hampered by this massive load?

Yes, we are. Because, you see, Samson was actually manipulating a threshold covenant for his own protection. While he was inside the city of Gaza, he was protected by a threshold covenant. This was why the Philistines didn't rush him at the prostitute's house but waited *outside* the gate. Their plan was once he was back outside the city and no longer covered by the threshold covenant, he was fair game. But Samson took hold of the city gates and, as he moved with them, he extended the boundaries of the city. He kept going until he was in sight of Hebron—an Israelite city of refuge—where the town guards no doubt would have rushed to his defence.

It was a clever trick.

But we reap what we sow. The trickster was about to be tricked. Over a woman. And when he was taken captive, he was brought to—where else?—Gaza. Where he died between two pillars.

The final act of his life was a reaping of his previous threshold covenant violation. And it sets the scene for the next pair of stories. Having established that the only good Philistine is a dead Philistine and that they are treacherous villains—one and all, man and woman—the writer pulls out a final twist: actually, by comparison with the Israelites, the Philistines are the absolute epitome of virtue. They wouldn't dream of violating a threshold covenant. But such is not the case with the Israelites—who, more than any other nation, should demonstrate integrity in this regard. After all, the 'master threshold covenant', as it were, is the Passover of God.

The thorns which I have reap'd are of the tree
I planted; they have torn me, and I bleed.
I should have known what fruit would spring from such a seed.
                                    Lord Byron, *Childe Harold's Pilgrimage*

The style of story-telling in the final two tales—which apparently involve the same person—is like a modern crime mystery: drop some obvious hints and clues, spike the tension with some serious shocks, then throw in a major twist.

Okay, spoiler alert. The person who links these final stories together is Jonathan, the son of Gershom, the son of Moses. Many commentators[70] note that the scribes were so reluctant to reveal the identity of Jonathan's grandfather they concealed his name, rendering it as 'Manasseh'. However they didn't conceal it very well: in fact, they highlighted it by creating an unusual textual feature. The difference between Moses and Manasseh in written Hebrew is simply a letter 'n', *nun*. But this 'n' is not inserted, it is positioned above the name Moses. 'Manasseh' means *forgetfulness* and this tiny 'n' superscript showed that Jonathan had totally forgotten the ways of his grandfather.

Now, don't get mixed up here with Jonathan, son of Saul. They are completely different people, from completely different tribes, in completely different time eras. However, it's no coincidence they share a name. Way back in the first chapter, I pointed out that families tend to name their children for the unresolved issue in their ancestral line.

Two or three generations down the track from this grandson of Moses, a hundred years or more after the incidents in the story take place, Saul's family was still contending with one unresolved issue: implacable hatred of a man named Jonathan. A man whose actions were responsible for the destruction of almost an entire tribe.

Now this first Jonathan was a Levite, as his grandfather had been. He was not one of the judges. He settled in Bethlehem.[71] He married a local woman, probably as his second wife, since she is termed his 'concubine'.[72] Chances are, given the time period of this story, she was related to Boaz and Ruth. If not, she would have been known to them.

For unspecified reasons—perhaps to visit his cousin, the High Priest Eleazar—Jonathan goes to the hill country of Ephraim. There, in search of a place to stay, he encounters a shady character named Micah. In the backstory Micah had stolen a fortune in silver from his mother and, fearful of the curses he heard her pronouncing on the thief, he had admitted to the robbery. She comes up with a cunning plan to make sure he doesn't steal the silver again—she gives it to him to be made into an idol. Soon he's also got an ephod—no doubt copied from Eleazar, since he lived in the general vicinity—and a set of household gods.

His unusual home decor soon attracted the wrong sort of

attention. But, before it did, Jonathan came wandering past. Micah, on realising he was a Levite, decided he'd be a much nicer status symbol than his own son.

Jonathan agreed to be priest-for-hire.

At this time in the story, his identity has not been revealed. He is consistently called 'the young Levite'. Some time later, some spies from the tribe of Dan are on their way north to conquer new territory. As they were passing by Micah's place, they recognised the young Levite's voice and called in to ask him what he was doing there.

Their surprise, their earnest questions, their desire for the sort of guidance which should more properly have come from the High Priest, should alert us to the fact this anonymous young Levite is someone of significance. Where on earth could they have become familiar enough with the sound of his voice to instantly recognise it?

The writer leaves us in suspense for a while, only revealing Jonathan's identity after the spies return home, gather up the whole tribe and—once more passing Micah's home—persuade Jonathan to steal the idols and the ephod as well as the household gods and come along with them.

Micah has reaped what he sowed. The tribe of Dan have acquired a priest of their own with a high priest's ephod. Jonathan in effect usurped the role of the high priest—his cousin—while his sons went on to set up the sanctuary at the town of Dan with a pair of golden calves.

Yes, the grandson of Moses is responsible for repeating the very same sin of idolatry in the very same way that had caused his grandfather such heartache. This is the sin that should have passed down Aaron's line; not the line of Moses! What caused the shift? How did it slide across family lines? Good question, and one we'll look at later.

The writer's comment about the golden calves is effectively the finale of the story, but we've missed the entire middle section. The writer has deliberately played with the chronology so that the horrifying climax of threshold covenant violation is reserved until last. How on earth *did* those spies recognise Jonathan's voice? Where could he have been and what could he have done that would make his voice familiar?

The story that follows this one is the last in the book of Judges. It too is about an anonymous Levite from Bethlehem who goes to the hill country of Ephraim. Implied throughout the narrative is that this is Jonathan again. In it is the explanation as to why the men of Dan recognised his voice. He'd called the tribes to war; arranging an assembly and then standing before them exhorting vengeance. And it was not against an external enemy that he'd campaigned but against one of their own. It wasn't the Moabites, the Midianites, the Ammonites or the Philistines that were the object of his rallying cry—it was the tribe of Benjamin.

Jonathan was the man who destroyed the unity of the tribes that his grandfather had tried so hard to build. The brotherhood that Moses had spent forty years forging in the crucible of the desert was blown away in a single instant through the action of his grandson.

We have learned to fly the air like birds and swim the sea like fish, but we have not learned the simple art of living together as brothers.
Martin Luther King, Jr., *Strength to Love*

There's a Scriptural verse I often hear people quote about how to build an understanding of God's Word. Whenever I hear this particular line, I wait to see if they're going to go right to the end. *'And the word of the Lord will be to them precept upon precept, precept upon precept, line upon line, line upon line...'* (Isaiah 28:13 ESV)

Sounds good, you might think. What's wrong with that? Build up your knowledge and understanding a little at a time.

Let's look at the full verse, however. *'And the word of the Lord will be to them precept upon precept, precept upon precept, line upon line, line upon line, here a little, there a little, that they may go, and fall backward, and be broken, and snared, and taken.'* (Isaiah 28:13 ESV)

In context, this isn't an exhortation about how to deepen your understanding of the word of God. It's a warning about what *not* to do. As a couple of friends of mine quipped: when you take the text out of the context, all you've got left is a con.

Irony of ironies, when this verse is truncated it's used to promote the very thing it alerts us to avoid. When you build an edifice of knowledge about Scripture by picking a verse from here and a verse from there, you will not only fall backward into a spiritual snare, you will—as the next verses indicate—set up false refuges for yourself and participate in a covenant with death.

To look, in isolation, at the story of how Moses' grandson destroyed the tribal alliance is to miss its true relevance. It's also to miss the reasons why for one of the most exquisitely beautiful stories of Jesus' life.

So first we'll look at the text and then at the context.

Jonathan's concubine gets really angry with him. Quite a few texts say she was unfaithful or 'played the harlot', however the rabbinic commentary on the Hebrew simply remarks she was incredibly angry. Enough to leave him and go back to her father's house in Bethlehem. And let's face it—she had good reason, quite apart from any domestic issues. Jonathan was a Levite but to wear an ephod was to usurp the role of the high priest. It was to set himself up in opposition to his own cousin. It was to create the potential for huge tension not only in the hill country of Ephraim, but throughout all of Israel.

His action in accepting what Micah offered is an indication of a huge lack of integrity—and perhaps of deep-seated jealousy. After all, every year his cousin got to preside over the great festivals. The house of Aaron was a prominent star amongst the people, but the house of Moses had slipped into shadowy obscurity.

Anyway, the concubine left. After several months, the Levite travelled to Bethlehem to woo her back. His father-in-law turns out to be an exceptionally generous man. (Now perhaps Bethlehem was a town of exceptionally generous men or perhaps it would not be amiss to suggest this unnamed man is Boaz or a close relative. It would be around the right time period, after all.) He shows his generosity through his hospitality—five days of it.

Now in Bedouin culture, hospitality is still a feature of a campsite. Any guest, even a perfect stranger, may arrive and be granted a welcome for three full days. Food, drink and shelter will be offered without any questions being asked or demands being made. However, after three days, polite and subtle inquiries will be made about the guest's intentions. How long does he expect to stay? How can he begin to contribute to the camp?

The free ride doesn't go on indefinitely.

I've made inquiries through friends who know some rabbis in Israel. Does the extended description of the father-in-law's hospitality on days four and five suggest the Levite is taking advantage of a free ride? They've assured me 'no'—that the passage merely indicates how generous the father-in-law's nature is. I'm not entirely convinced that's all the verses indicate. Tola and Jair in Judges 10 get their entire lives summed up in less space than it takes to describe two days of entertaining this Levite in Bethlehem.

In fact, these five verses are so detailed they are obviously making some significant point that is not covered by a simple statement like: 'The generous father-in-law prevailed on the Levite to stay five days.'

One obvious point is that, because of the meal-sharing, a threshold covenant exists between Jonathan and his father-in-law. Now, to a degree, this should be self-evident. However the writer may have wanted to spell it out in order to drive home a contrast with the upcoming threshold covenant violation.

In the afternoon of the fifth day, the Levite decides to leave. He takes his concubine and his servant and they set off towards the hill country of Ephraim. It's getting quite late when the servant suggests they seek shelter for the night in the walled fortress of the Jebusites—a place later to be conquered by David and become his capital, Jerusalem.[73] Jonathan dismisses the servant's suggestion and says he won't stay with unbelievers. Instead he orders that they push on to Gibeah or Ramah.

They reach Gibeah in the territory of Benjamin just as the sun is setting.

The people of the town aren't hospitable but an old man takes eventually them in. His welcome, because it includes eating together, indicates a threshold covenant was in place between himself and the party of travellers.

The house is surrounded by men who demand the Levite be sent out to them so they can satiate their sexual desires on him. The host—reflecting Lot's reaction in a similar situation in Sodom some six or seven hundred years previously—offers to send out his virgin daughter and the concubine. This old man was obligated by the requirements of threshold covenant to defend his guest to the death, which is why he offers up his daughter to assuage the men's lusts.

In fact, the obligation was mutual—the Levite was also required to defend him to the death. This may explain why the concubine was included in the offer.

She is the one sent out. After being gang-raped all night, she dies at dawn while reaching out her hand to touch the threshold.

Her action and the time at which it occurred say more than words can ever do. From beyond the gates of death, her voice speaks through this action: 'I am the threshold sacrifice.'

Not a lamb, not a goat, not a calf. A woman. A wife. She was violated by everyone in the story: the husband who ignored his threshold covenant of marriage with her, the host who ignored his threshold covenant of protection with her, the town who ignored its threshold covenant obligations to strangers.

By the end of Act 1 in this episode, the wonderful hospitality of a host in Bethlehem has given way to a shocking contrast in Gibeah.

Jonathan wastes no time. He cuts up her body and sends the twelve pieces around all the tribes. This grisly call to war was normally done with the pieces of a bullock.[74] The tribes assemble at Mizpah where Jonathan addresses them and tells the story of the atrocity at Gibeah. (Here at last we have the reason why the men of Dan recognised his voice: he'd called them to war and had addressed them in person.)

The whole assembly agrees that the men of Gibeah need to be punished for the crime. They send a message to the tribe of Benjamin to hand over the evil-doers. The men of Benjamin decide to defend the town instead.

So a war's on.

At first, the eleven tribes get whopped. Then they go to Bethel where Phinehas—son of Eleazar and Jonathan's second cousin—was ministering before the Ark of the Covenant. After consulting with God, they go out again. This time, the eleven tribes are the victors. Suddenly the territory of Benjamin becomes a vast killing field. The army wipes out every man, woman and child in Benjamin with the exception of six hundred men who escaped to the wilderness.

End of Act 2: Jonathan's decision to call for war over the threshold covenant violation in Gibeah precipitated the almost complete extermination of an entire tribe. The call for war was never meant to pit brother against brother but to bring allies together for mutual defence against an external enemy.

The eleven tribes are naturally appalled. They hadn't meant to wipe out the people of Benjamin—just teach them a lesson about the importance of hospitality and threshold covenants. Remind them of what happened to the people of Sodom.

The Israelites realise they are likely to be responsible for genocide. Although they'd become aware of the six hundred survivors, they'd also taken a vow never to allow their daughters to marry a man of Benjamin.

But wait! A solution presents itself. The assembly suddenly realises no one from the town of Jabesh Gilead answered the call to war. Nobody from that town took any vows. So, in an even more horrifying 'fix' of the situation, the Israelites wipe out the town of Jabesh Gilead, all except for the young girls who are given as trophies of war to the survivors of the tribe of Benjamin.

There aren't quite enough girls to go around so a kind of 'sanctioned abduction' of young women of marriageable age was permitted at a dance at Shiloh.

So the Book of Judges ends.

As the curtain falls, do we expect peace to reign in a fairytale happily-ever-after?

We already know from the previous section that Jonathan, the architect of this catastrophe, returned to the hill country of Ephraim and, from there, took up the invitation of the tribe of Dan to move to the far north. Well away from Bethlehem or Gibeah. Two places that might well have had very solid reasons for disliking, even hating, him.

And although the Book of Judges might have ended, the story is far from over.

What Jonathan wrought doesn't stop with the rebuilding of the tribe of Benjamin. Every man in the clan was a survivor of genocide, every woman a trophy of war.

Trauma like that doesn't disappear in a day. It goes on and on, through generation after generation.

No snowflake in an avalanche ever feels responsible.

Voltaire

The writer of the book of Judges framed his story to end on a note of hope. He played with the chronology of events to create a stylistic, suspenseful drama ending with the prospect of the tribe Benjamin rising from the ashes.

In the Christian bible, the next book is Ruth, while in Hebrew scrolls, the books of Samuel follow. 1 Samuel 1:1 LEB opens with: *'There was a certain man from Ramathaim Zophim, from the hill country of Ephraim...'*

Here's an immediate alert. The hill country of Ephraim was where Jonathan was heading when the atrocity in Gibeah occurred; there resided both Eleazar, the high priest, and his son Phinehas.

Already we should be clued into the fact the Book of Samuel is a continuation of the entwined traumas of threshold covenant violation, rape, murder, genocide, and abduction of young girls saved from the total annihilation of their town simply to be given to some survivors of genocide.

Yes, it's a new beginning.

But the past is still playing out. And it's very easy to overlook that. But, we should consider the modern science of epigenetics, which tells us that traumatic experiences suffered by our ancestors can leave molecular scars that adhere to our DNA. Survivors of catastrophic events carry more than just memories. Like a scaffold on the outside of a building, epigenetic markers temporarily fix themselves to our genetic structure. 'Temporarily' being three or four generations.

If you're reminded of the curse of the sins of the fathers from Exodus 20:5, you wouldn't be far wrong.

'I, the Lord your God, am a jealous God, punishing the children for the sin of the parents to the third and fourth generation of those who hate Me.'
Exodus 20:5 NIV

So does Scripture tell us anything about the second or third or fourth generation of the people of Gibeah, Bethlehem and the hill country of Ephraim? These people, after all, would be most affected by any curse. And Gibeah, having borne the brunt of the trauma, should be by far the worst.

Tick. Tick. Tick. Samuel from the hill country of Ephraim, Saul from Gibeah, David from Bethlehem.

God has called these three people to the same sort of tests that we saw in the story of Isaac and Abimelech. Just as Isaac was called to 'mend the world' by passing the test his father had twice failed, so Saul is called to 'mend the world' that the fathers in his hometown had failed.

This is not as simple a test as Isaac's; it involves:

- reconciling the people of Benjamin with a priest from the hill country of Ephraim
- reconciling the people of Israel with the people of the town of Jabesh Gilead
- reconciling the people of Gibeah with the people of Bethlehem

Tough tasks! But amazingly, despite the scars on his soul coming down from his parents or grandparents, Saul achieves the first two of them. That's a staggering accomplishment. Especially when we consider he comes from a line of people associated with the breaking of covenant. Is it any wonder, given the history of his family, he is subject to black moods, depression and fits of jealous rage? His father—or grandfather—was a survivor of genocide. His mother—or grandmother—was a trophy of war.

His friendship with Samuel is the means by which Saul passes the first test.[75]

His first action as king—saving the people of the rebuilt town of Jabesh Gilead—is the means by which he passes the second test.

But, on being faced with a boy from Bethlehem who could play the harp like an angel, slay giants and inspire unswerving loyalty in both men and women, all the latent generational hatred in Saul's line came to the fore. Along with his own brooding envy.

Saul's inability to pass the third test has immense ramifications. Instead of 'mending the world' by reconciling the people of his hometown with the people of Bethlehem, he sent the curse hurtling on down the generations. If he'd kept covenant with David, as his own son was to do, further tragedy might have been avoided.

The issue, of course, is covenant. Specifically, it's threshold covenant. And so, because we not only reap what we sow but we reap in the same kind as we sow, the issue of threshold covenant violation is about to repeat itself. And repeat itself.

We don't find out for sure until the end of the second book of Samuel how or where Saul commits the same sort of atrocity as has been committed against his own hometown of Gibeah. But right at the beginning of the second book, we are given a set of clues that should enable us to take a really good guess.

As the second book of Samuel opens, Saul has just died in battle. So has his son, Jonathan.

Some Israelites are backing Ish-bosheth, another of Saul's sons, as king—while some others are backing David.

David's forces, under the command of his nephew Joab, encounter Ish-bosheth's forces, under the command of Saul's cousin, Abner. These troops happen to cross each other's paths at the Pool of Gibeon.

One group sits on one side of the water and one on the other.

Now Abner and Joab are apparently good friends, despite being on opposite sides of the political divide. But Abner is a man of Benjamin, probably from Gibeah, and the spiritual defilement in his generation hasn't lifted yet. He calls out to Joab, 'Let's have a bit of fun! How about playing a threshold game?'

Now English translations of 2 Samuel 2:14 don't pick up on the word denoting *threshold* because it doesn't make much sense to interpreters. But because I'm tracing the effects of threshold covenant violation down the generations, I'm vitally interested in this particular word, 'shaq'. Meaning both *laugh* and *lintel,* and alluding to *watchmen* and *first awakenings*, it's a word related to the name Isaac.

In this threshold game, two sets of twelve combatants pair off. They grab each other by the hair and stab each other in the side.

And, not surprisingly, they all fall down dead.

What on earth possessed Abner to suggest this? And what on earth possessed Joab to agree to it?

What unholy spirits were defiling the Pool of Gibeon?

The clues are all there. Abner uses a word related to a *threshold*.

Just as a woman of Bethlehem was sacrificed on a threshold and cut into twelve pieces, so too are twelve Benjaminites and twelve of David's men sacrificed on a threshold.

When Abner tries to escape the ensuing battle, he is pursued by Asahel of Bethlehem. Asahel is Joab's brother and the son of Zeruiah, David's sister. Asahel is killed and the conflict between Bethlehem and Gibeah goes on.

Of course, we find out much later that the Pool of Gibeon is the site of a massacre. Saul, doomed by his own judgments to perpetuate vengeance where he had failed to forgive, has all but exterminated the Gibeonites.

Centuries previously, the Gibeonites had tricked Joshua into a covenant. It wasn't strictly a threshold covenant but, being the first covenant in the Promised Land, it had similar overtones.

Saul's attempt at genocide not only reflects the virtual genocide of his own tribe, it also mirrors covenant violation. Just to make sure the parallel is obvious, we should note that 'Gibeon' has the same meaning as 'Gibeah'.

If we didn't know the land was defiled by simply noting the bizarreness of the threshold game at the Pool of Gibeon, it's finally spelled out for us in 2 Samuel 21:

During the reign of David, there was a famine for three successive years; so David sought the face of the Lord. The Lord said, "It is on account of Saul and his blood-stained house; it is because he put the Gibeonites to death." The king summoned the Gibeonites and spoke to them. (Now the Gibeonites were not a part of Israel but were survivors of the Amorites; the Israelites had sworn to spare them, but Saul in his zeal for Israel and Judah had tried to annihilate them.) David asked the Gibeonites, "What shall I do for you? How shall I make atonement so that you will bless the Lord's inheritance?... What do you want me to do for you?"

They answered the king, "As for the man who destroyed us and plotted against us so that we have been decimated and have no place anywhere in

Israel, let seven of his male descendants be given to us to be killed and their bodies exposed before the Lord at Gibeah of Saul—the Lord's chosen one."

So the king said, "I will give them to you."
2 Samuel 21:1-6 NIV

Bad choice. Really bad choice.

David was in covenant with both Saul and Jonathan. He's supposed to take care of their families for as long as he lives. He's supposed to defend these men, not turn them over to the Gibeonites.

And although he does turn them over for execution, he eventually comes to repent of his own covenant violation.

So did David's repentance end this cycle forever?

My guess is no, it didn't.

Sure, God began to answer prayer on behalf of the land and the famine lifted, but the final healing of the nation seems to me to have still been a thousand years in the future.

Before Jesus went to His Father, just after His resurrection, He reversed the curse of Eden while in the garden with Mary Magdalene. In Eden, God went seeking the whereabouts of humanity but, in the garden outside the tomb, humanity went seeking the whereabouts of God.

However, when Jesus returned from heaven that same day, the top of His priority list was obviously not to comfort His mother and reassure His disciples. If reversing the curse of Eden was first, what was the next most devastating event in Israelite history? Apparently it was the threshold covenant violation in Gibeah of Benjamin.

The destruction of the tribal brotherhood, the defilement of the land and people, the bloodshed that went on for generations all began with a man and a woman on the road to Gibeah of Benjamin.

Emmaus was on that same road.

'Independence'... middle-class blasphemy. We are all dependent on one another, every soul... on earth.

G.B. Shaw, *Pygmalion*

Healing the land, mending history, repairing the world. That's the meaning of passing a test our forbears have failed. *God fixes*, just as Jonathan's name says.

And He calls us to be part of this divine restoration.

The book of Judges is not a place we'd expect to find a schism in relationships second only to the sin of Eden. It's a book we tend to overlook as we scoot towards the tales of the great kings.

But Israel was never supposed to have a king.

Even when God allowed it, the taint was already in place: the people acclaimed Saul, probably because his tribe was so small. Benjamin could never lord it over the others.

And, just as the land of Israel was cursed by the threshold covenant violation at Gibeah, so our modern nations have been defiled by the actions of our ancestors.

In the land of my birth, Australia, I am saddened to realise the destruction of the bora rings of our first peoples reflects a similar threshold covenant violation. The word 'bora' is an eastern Australian dialect; a truncation of 'kipparah'.[76] I hope you recognise the similarity between this ancient aboriginal word and the Hebrew for a *sanctified threshold*.

The rituals performed at a bora ring have the marks of 'blood covenant' written all over them.

How can we bless the defiled land? How can we speak healing into the violated earth? The story of Jesus on the road to Emmaus shows us that it doesn't have to be full of fanfare. The early Christians realised the story of Jesus joining Cleopas and his unnamed companion was about the Levite and his concubine and adapted translations accordingly. The *Codex*

Alexandrinus altered the Greek text of Judges 19:9 so that it reads just like Luke 24:29. According to Carsten Thiede, most modern translators have seen the parallel too and given the verses identical wording.[77]

The story of Emmaus shows us that actions are necessary. Actions which bring Jesus into the heart of the reparation.

Because, at the end of the day, it's all too easy to blame the wrong person. Without Jesus and the Holy Spirit as our legal advocate, we might ask for healing that addresses the atrocity, rather than the heart issues that caused it.

It might seem that a toxic seed sprang up in the heart of Jonathan the Levite and caused such a catastrophic division in Israel that eventually God ignored prayer on behalf of the land.

But it's not as simple as that. The problem, in my view, doesn't start with Jonathan. It starts with Moses.

God offered Moses a name covenant and he refused. Then he added an insult: he undertook a treacherous threshold covenant and was only saved from death by his wife. By circumcising someone—it could have been Moses himself or one of their sons, Gershom or Eleazar—she turned the situation around. The lack of circumcision indicates a lack of covenant commitment.[78]

The attack by God must have been incredibly traumatic. Zipporah, in saving the situation, throws a foreskin at Moses' feet and tells him he is a 'bridegroom of blood'.

God takes His covenant seals incredibly seriously.

What is a seal? It's a sign of covenant.

The seal of the blood covenant with Noah was a rainbow.

The seal of the name covenant with Abraham was circumcision.

The seal of the threshold covenant with Israel through Moses was the Sabbath.

The seal of the salt covenant with David was the temple.

All very different; all very significant.[79]

Now the satan counterfeits the works of God. He has covenants too. With seals.

The consequences of breaking ungodly covenants are just as serious as when Moses effectively spat in God's face by refusing to display the sign of a godly covenant. In the days of the early church, Ananias and Sapphira[80] do a similar thing: the seal of the new covenant is the Holy Spirit. And they lie to Him, about Him, and in spite of Him.

Seals have the potential to be deadly. And, but for the amazing grace and mercy of God when it comes to satanic seals, most of us would be dead. The satan booby-traps his seals because he doesn't want us to repudiate the covenants our ancestors have taken out with him. Should we discover one and do away with it through prayer, that very action may trigger the explosive opening of another seal. So don't rush into removing your seals: ask the Holy Spirit to reveal them all—there can be up to seven of them—and when you've found them, ask Jesus to deal with them. He is the only one who can safely deal with both ungodly seals and ungodly covenants.

He is the only one who can intervene to cut off, through the power of His cross, the reaping we are due because of what we've sowed. Or because of what our generations have sowed.

Moses was the original 'bridegroom of blood'. In the traumatic moment when God tried to kill him, what was written into his son's heart? I believe it was this:

- Undertaking threshold covenants with unbelievers is potentially fatal.
- God won't defend you in a lodging place; He may be your adversary.
- The wife's actions will mean the difference between life and death for the husband.

As we reflect on the story of Jonathan, the third generation from Moses, we see epigenetic reactions in play. He dismisses the possibility of staying with the Jebusites, although it's clear from the story of Samson that unbelievers do acknowledge the sanctity of the threshold covenant. Although he is a Levite, there's no indication he called on God for help—instead he expects his concubine will divert the attention of the attackers. The surprise is that she does: the focus of the violence turns away from him. This tends to indicate the direction of his spiritual expectations, confirming his heart's belief that, once the woman was involved, the direct assault on himself would end.

Jonathan takes 'bridegroom of blood' to an entirely different level as the defilements of his generational line spill over from sacrificing his bride to a call for war to triggering a genocide which in turn activated another and another—ending up, in the time of David, with famine and starvation.

Yet, Jesus takes 'bridegroom of blood' to the ultimate level. He inverts it; sacrificing His life for His bride, not only keeping covenant but also creating a new one in His blood. That He is the bridegroom who gives birth to the bride is reiterated in a multiplication of subtle ways throughout John's gospel.[81]

I'm not sure Moses ever repented of his threshold covenant violation. My reason is: God didn't allow him into the Promised Land. This, of course, was because, when the people were grumbling about a lack of water—yet *again!*—Moses struck a rock to produce the flow. God had told him and Aaron to *speak* to the rock, not *strike* it.

God seems fussy, pedantic and snappishly hard-to-please in this episode. But is He? It takes place forty years after Moses had betrayed God on the way to Egypt. Now threshold covenant is all about stones. Cornerstones, to be precise.

If you pass over them, you come into covenant.
If you strike them, you refuse the covenant.
If you pass over the stone, you honour the host.
If you strike the stone, you insult the host.

So there was God, offering water as a good host would, and what did Moses do? He insulted God before the entire assembly. He struck a rock—symbolic of repudiating a covenant.

Now, it's true the rock in question was not a threshold stone. But it's also true the purpose for standing before the rock was to *draw water*. An action directly related to the name Moses, *drawn from the water*.

In effect, this is the God-of-second-chances giving Moses a second chance at name covenant. And it's Moses turning Him down once more. Despite everything that's happened in the past forty years, despite God's unparalleled record of faithfulness and provision and miraculous deliverance, Moses is still unwilling to fully trust Him. Some corner of his heart is still in conflict with the Almighty.

Now it's one thing to lash out at God in private but it's entirely another in public. All the multitude of witnesses, waiting for water, knew what the action of striking a stone meant. They knew it was a repudiation of covenant.

They knew why the Egyptians had suffered the fate they did: because they were not in covenant with Yahweh—they had, as Exodus 12:23 suggests, not passed over but instead had dashed their foot against the cornerstone.[82]

God had made it clear through the Passover (passing over a threshold stone) that He was their covenant defender. The Egyptians had struck the stone, stumbling against it and thereby refusing the covenant.

'Moses, when he grew up, refused to be called the son of Pharaoh's daughter... He thought it was better to suffer... than to own the treasures of Egypt, for he was looking ahead to his great reward.' (Hebrews 11:24–26 NLT)

True! But sometimes the heart is in conflict. Apparently, despite this 'looking ahead', some core aspect of Moses' identity was still in solidarity with the Egyptians and he wasn't going to tamper with the name that came from that culture. Even eighty years after fleeing the country for defending an Israelite slave!

So, like the Egyptians reaping what they had sown, Moses reaped what he'd sown. He refused the name covenant and threshold covenant of God; God therefore refused to allow him to make the passage over the threshold into the Promised Land.

When a pattern of trouble strikes and the same kind of repeated issues make life unmanageable, it's worth looking closer at the basic principles which hold true across all Scripture. *Sowing and reaping* is the most consistent spiritual law of all.[83] The Israelites were slaves in Egypt because they reaped what their forefathers had sown. Their great-grandfathers had sold Joseph into Egypt—and despite Joseph's attempts, they hadn't reconciled with him. Some people think the law of sowing and reaping has been cancelled by the death of Jesus on the cross but, in Galatians 6:7, Paul assures us that we reap what we sow.

The Egyptians had reaped what they sowed. Around the time Moses was born, the reigning Pharaoh ordered his people to throw newborn boys into the river Nile. The reaping came to pass when the armies of Egypt were overthrown in the waters of the Sea.

The only reason reaping is so hard to spot in Scripture is because it is often so far removed in time from the initial sowing. A good reason for it to be called 'reaping'! The consequences are not immediate but follow a season of growth—sometimes decades of it. Our lives become like fields full of thorns and thistles and we don't even know where to begin to clean it up.

The second most significant Biblical principle is that of multiplication: *sow the wind, reap the whirlwind*. The longer an issue remains unresolved, the greater the reaping will be. If it passes from one generation to the next, a small storm will have become a line of vicious tornadoes.

The third principle: *honour everyone*. No exceptions. Many people think that it's not only fine but our duty to curse the satan and revile his minions. This, as indicated previously, is a violation of the injunctions in 2 Peter 2:13 and Jude 1:9-11. Some people think that, despite this Scripture, they still have authority to hurl abuse at the powers of darkness. I do not hold that God will confer on anyone, even Himself, the right to go against His own Word.

After all, Scripture says He has magnified His Word even above His name. (Psalm 138:2)

Furthermore, it's a waste of time addressing the satan when those moments could be spent in intimacy with God.

A corollary to this principle is honour your father and mother, that it may go well with you in life. (Exodus 20:12; Ephesians 6:2-3) Conversely, if it isn't going well with you, it is good to pose a question to the Lord: 'How did I dishonour my father and mother? When? How long ago?'

The fourth principle: *all these curses can be made null and void at the Cross.* But the grace God supplied at the Cross must be applied in our lives. It's all about provision for intimacy and relationship: the Cross is not a push-button automatic reset to a default righteousness. It's about walking hand in hand with Jesus and stopping occasionally for radical open-heart surgery.

These principles operate by impartial law—they apply to both kinds of threshold stones: the sanctified kaph and the defiled miphtan.

These principles are not curses. The principle of sowing and reaping is designed to be a blessing. We sow blessings into the lives of others, we reap blessings—multiplied many times.

God treats us with amazing dignity: He bestows on us the right to determine the standard we will be judged by, along with the measure of blessing we'll receive in life.

He doesn't choose our level of reward. We do.

6

A Comparison of Cousins

THE CURIOUS RELATIONSHIP BETWEEN THE NAMES, Levi and Leviathan, spreads its tentacles into the name Jonathan. Levi means *join* or *joined to* and Leviathan, *joined sea-monster*—perhaps referring to the shields tightly so sealed together on its back no air can pass between them.[84] Totally unnoticed, however, in all reference works I've consulted is that the element for *sea-monster* also occurs at the back-end of the name, Jonathan.

Certainly, Jonathan means *God gives* or *God appoints* or *God fixes*, but hidden deep within the name is a darker choice: *hand of the sea-monster*. Jonathan's path forked at Gibeah: he could have looked to God or he could have become like the twisting serpent of the deep. It was his choice to become more like the creature than the Creator. He came to embody a spirit of backlash and payback and, in doing so, he set out to punish dishonour disproportionately and became puffed up like the dragon-king of the sons of pride.

A latently brutal nature, lashing out in violence, emerged in Jonathan's behaviour after the death of his concubine at Gibeah.

Contrast him with his second cousin, Phinehas.

It's the proverbial chalk and cheese.

Yet, if Jonathan has *hand of the sea-monster* hidden as a possibility in his name, Phinehas hasn't fared any better. His name is often translated as *mouth of brass*. However the 'nehas' which finishes his name is the same element as is found at the start of Nehushtan.

This was the brass serpent Moses raised up on a pole in the desert;

the prophetic healing symbol of Jesus lifted up on the Cross.[85] The ending 'tan' of the word is identical to the '–than' of Leviathan and Jonathan, and comes from 'tanniyn' meaning *sea-monster*. The first element, 'nehas', can be rendered as *burning serpent* and is used to describe a seraph.

So Phinehas means *mouth of the burning serpent* with a built-in symphonic resonance: *voice of the seraph*.

If Jonathan is the *hand of the serpent*, Phinehas is the *jaws*.

At first sight it seems strange that both cousins seem named after some sea-monster. But perhaps it's not so odd. Psalm 74:14 NKJV in discussing God's redemption of the people of Israel from Egypt says: 'You broke the heads of Leviathan in pieces, and gave him as food to the people[86] inhabiting the wilderness.'

The wonder of this event must have stayed within the memory of the people for years. Children born in the wilderness years were named for God's triumph over the spirits of the threshold as well as the monstrous serpents that symbolised them.

So these names commemorate an act of marvellous provision after a spectacular rescue from the Egyptian armies.

The episode in which Phinehas features most prominently has to be one of the most significant, as well as the most underrated, in Scripture. Peculiar clues are embedded in the text, highlighting the importance of the episode in salvation history. These oddities include a disparity in the spelling of Phinehas' name, perhaps indicating a name covenant with God; and a singular exception to the iron-clad scribal rule forbidding the breaking of letters.

This episode involving Phinehas is, of course, all about threshold covenant. And it probably tells us more about how defilement works and also how to overcome it than any other place in Scripture.

We first hear of Phinehas in Exodus 6:25 where it is simply noted his father is Eleazar and his mother a daughter of Putiel. He next appears in Numbers 25:7 with a spear in his hand. As far as dramatic entrances go, he's probably cornered the market.

A plague is ravaging the Israelite campsite; 24000 people have died as the result of a curse which has come upon the people because of their idolatry and worship of Baal Peor. The Israelites are weeping and repenting before God when Zimri, a prince of the tribe of Simeon, saunters into the camp, flaunting his liaison with Cozbi, a Midianite princess.

Outraged, Phinehas takes his spear and follows Zimri and Cozbi into a tent and kills them both with a single spear-thrust through the belly. The plague stops; God commends Phinehas for his zeal and confers on him an everlasting priesthood with an accompanying covenant of peace.

These are the bare bones of the story you'll find in any English translation. It's a passage I struggled with for a very long time, because the God of this passage seems to reward the very thing He's just commanded the Israelites to avoid: murder. His praise for Phinehas not only seems inappropriate but disproportionate as well.

God is holy, no doubt about it, but He's also merciful. If we were to take this story at face value, it would be a licence to slay anyone who offends against the sanctity of His name. Which happens to be all of us, at some time or another.

Now, because the background of this story is threshold covenant, hedged with more threshold covenant and ringed about with yet more threshold covenant, the spiritual implications for passing over into our destiny are enormous. I wrestled for many months with the significance of the broken letter and the change in Phinehas' name in this passage.

To understand it, let's back up a moment and take a long view of the circumstances surrounding the event.

The Israelites are almost at the end of their wilderness wanderings. All but two of an entire generation of men has died; the people are on the threshold of the Promised Land once more. Arriving on the west bank of the Jordan River, they camp in the Valley of Acacias. Perhaps not the wisest choice—this is the ancient site of the city of Sodom, the place where Scripture records the very first threshold covenant violation. They made the choice to pitch their tents in a long-defiled landscape. And they should have known better. The Hebrew word for *acacia* is related to *turn aside*. That was the message of the valley: go elsewhere.

But they didn't. They stayed where they were and, observing them arrayed in their tribal units from the heights above, was the king of Moab and his court, along with the diviner Balaam from Pethor.

If you recognised 'Pethor' as belonging to the family of words which include 'miphtan', 'Jephthah' and 'pethen', you'd be right. Pethor is variously translated as *opening*, *prophetic utterances* or *interpret dreams*[87] and was long considered to be the site of an oracular temple and synonymous with the Jordanian city of Petra.

Some eight hundred years before the Greek shrine of Delphi was established, settling firmly in people's minds that Python and the spirit of divination were one and the same, the Hebrew people already knew of the link. They also knew Python was a constricting threshold guardian, a 'god' of openings and doorways.

Now Balaam was hired by the king of Moab to curse the people of Israel. Somewhat ironically, his donkey turns out to be an oracular seer surpassing Balaam himself. The donkey notices an angel with a sword, and tries to avoid it. Now, as I've pointed out before, angels and thresholds go together.

Balaam eventually gets God's message that his prophecies cannot curse Israel. The king of Moab is decidedly unimpressed when not once, but three times, Balaam delivers words of prosperity over them. It's clear that, had Balaam not held a sacred office of diviner and dream interpreter, he'd have come to a nasty end then and there.

Balaam effectively disappears from the foreground of the story. It is only revealed much later that, to get his pay from the king of Moab, he counselled a very different kind of strategy—to entice the Israelites into idolatry so that God's protection would be removed from them. When it became clear to Balaam that God was not going to break covenant with His people, the only other option was to get the people to break covenant with God. Covenants generally come with automatic curses for breaking them—and if God intervened in stopping those particular curses, He'd be violating His own word. If He were indeed a God of truth, unlike the capricious, lascivious gods roundabout, He'd have to keep *His* vows. But His protection would have to be lifted, if the Israelites broke *their* vows.

The strategy worked a treat. Some local ladies were sent in to seduce the Israelites and it didn't take long before men like Zimri were engaged in ritual prostitution. The purpose of such prostitution is to 'become one' with the god—in this case Baal Peor, *the god of the opening.*

Yes, *opening*: another threshold indicator.

The purpose of covenant is to 'become one'. Ritual prostitution is one of the counterfeits of covenant. In 'becoming one' with Baal Peor, the Israelites forfeited Yahweh's covenantal protection over them.

Effectively, metaphorically, they dashed their foot against the threshold stone. They 'stumbled' over it. Revelation 2:14 NAS spells out the parallel sin of a later age: *'you have there some who hold the teaching of Balaam, who... put a stumbling block before the sons of Israel...'*

As a consequence, plague ravaged its way through the tribes.

The Hebrew word here for *plague*, 'maggephah', comes from 'nagaph', *strike*. This is invariably used to describe the action of refusing a covenant by striking or dashing a foot against a threshold stone.

By breaking covenant with God, the people lost His covenantal defence. In effect, God says, 'You're on your own now. You've chosen Baal Peor, so let him protect you.' It's not so much that God sends the plague as He withdraws the guard keeping it at bay. As a result, 24000 people die.

The leaders are repenting, standing in the doorway of the Tabernacle (another threshold image) when Zimri goes past with Cozbi. Phinehas, whom later genealogies[88] reveal was the official in charge of the gatekeepers (another threshold motif) makes a swift decision. He takes a spear, goes into the tent after Zimri and Cozbi and kills them.

The New Revised Standard version is a fairly typical translation:

'*he went after the Israelite man into the tent, and pierced the two of them, the Israelite and the woman, through the belly. So the plague was stopped...*' (Numbers 25:8 NRS)

God then commends Phinehas: '*Phinehas son of Eleazar, the son of Aaron, the priest, has turned My anger away from the Israelites. Since he was as zealous for My honour among them as I am, I did not put an end to them in my zeal. Therefore tell him I am making my covenant of peace with him.*' (Numbers 25:11-12 NIV)

That word, *peace*—'shalom'—contains an anomaly. Hebrew scribes are expressly forbidden to break letters as they copy the Scriptures. But here, in the vav of 'shalom', they are not only allowed to insert a break but ordered to do so. The broken vav looks like a hand with a spear: fitting for what Phinehas did.

But a hand with a spear and a covenant of peace is, of course, prophetic of the death of Jesus. The spear in the side of Jesus is the moment of breaking the waters for the birth of the Bride of Christ.[89] It is Jesus who is our peace and our Passover, inaugurated through His new covenant.

How on earth can the murder of two people be a foreshadowing of the Cross? Sure and without question, Zimri and Cozbi are guilty but, when it comes to sin, so are we all. Doesn't Phinehas sin himself in killing them? Isn't he breaking the Law? So why does God not only let him off the hook but bless him? If this is how God metes out justice, I don't get it. And why does the passage suggest his actions are prophetic of the Messiah?

I wrangled with this puzzle for months until I realised that the translation '*he went after the Israelite man into the tent*' from Numbers 25:8 is deficient. Seriously so.

'*He went after the Israelite man into the tent*': over fifty English translations use *tent* for the original text's 'qubbah'. Some archaic versions use *whorehouse* or *brothel* but that's just as much an interpretation as *tent* is. The word 'qubbah' is uniquely translated *tent* in this verse. It's fundamentally the same as 'qabbah' meaning *curse*—the same word used by the king of Moab when he hired Balaam to fling maledictions at the Israelites.

Phinehas didn't so much enter the *tent* as he entered the *curse*.

A single word change and the whole passage unfolds with new meaning and makes perfect sense. Phinehas, like Jesus, voluntarily became a curse so that the people of Israel might have life. As Jesus offered eternal life through a covenant of peace, so Phinehas gave life to the Israelites through his action. He knew the Law. He knew the command against murder. He knew his own life was forfeit but he was willing to make the sacrifice. The choice was clear: stand by while the death toll rose or stop the plague with the sacrifice of Zimri, Cozbi and himself.

Here, laid bare, is the incredible difference between Phinehas and his cousin, Jonathan.

Phinehas was willing to die for the people. Jonathan preferred others die for him.

Phinehas was willing to enter a curse. Jonathan preferred the curse to fall on others.

Phinehas was willing suffer dishonour and disgrace. Jonathan preferred to avenge dishonour and disgrace.

Phinehas judged sin but was willing to step into the place of judgment and have justice executed upon himself. Not so with Jonathan.

The closer you look at Phinehas, the more like Jesus he is.

His zeal, like that of Jesus for the holiness of God, is tempered with a self-sacrificial desire to save lives.

He was given a covenant of peace and an everlasting priesthood.[90] Sound familiar? It should. Jesus not only is a priest forever after the order of Melchizedek (Hebrews 7:17), he is also a priest forever after the order of Phinehas.

Now not every covenant in Scripture is unconditional. Some

are, some aren't. Phinehas' covenant of peace is one of the absolute ones—just like the covenant God swore to Noah. No qualifications, no restrictions, no limitations. The seal of the covenant to Noah was the rainbow in the clouds, a mysterious symbol to Israel because the Divine Archer always had His bow pointed at His own heart. It is only in the life of Jesus we can understand this strange motif.

It's difficult to be sure what the seal of the covenant of peace is but I suspect it is that broken vav—the letter split so it looks like a hand with a spear. That hand is not just a prophecy of Jesus, but a hand lifted as much against Phinehas himself as it ever was against Zimri and Cozbi.

Jonathan is quite different. In contrast to the everlasting priesthood God granted to Phinehas, Jonathan created a position of hereditary high priesthood for his family. He did this by taking the opportunity presented by the tribe of Dan to set up a sanctuary in the far north. And, far from bringing a covenant of peace as his gift to the people, he persuaded the Israelites to destroy the tribal alliance and, in addition, to make vows that led to the almost total annihilation of the tribe of Benjamin.

The cousins are such complete contrasts that the inevitable question arises: was Jonathan jealous of Phinehas?

I'd say almost certainly. I'd say it, because it would be psychologically plausible and spiritually almost inevitable, given the high status Phinehas acquired and the fact he overcame the spirit of Python at a very critical moment.

If we list the markers we've noted so far connected with doors, gates or threshold covenants, there are:
1. the appearance of an angel in the story of Balaam
2. the place of origin of Balaam—a town called Pethor, meaning either *opening* or *divination/dream-interpretation*, both of which are connected to Python
3. the seduction of Baal Peor, *the god of the opening*
4. the repentance of the leaders in the doorway of the Tabernacle

5. it is recorded in Chronicles that Phinehas is the chief gatekeeper
6. the word for 'plague' is derived from a word for rejecting a threshold covenant
7. the Israelites are camped near the ancient site of Sodom, historically associated with the first threshold covenant violation on record
8. the Israelites are on the verge of a huge threshold—entering the Promised Land after forty years in the wilderness

All of these threshold indicators point to the fact that, in making the choice he did, Phinehas overcame the spiritual dynamic operative in the Valley of Acacias. He crushed Python the constrictor. Phinehas was part of the fulfilment of God's prophecy to the serpent in Genesis 3:15, *'I will put enmity between you and the woman, and between your offspring and hers; he will crush your head, and you will strike his heel.'*

The Greeks, about a millennium later, knew Python as a spirit of divination. However they had an additional insight that bears on the situation in the Valley of Acacias and the relationship between Phinehas and Jonathan. The Greek word for *envy* was 'phthónos' which was related to 'phtheírō', *decay, rot or corrupt,* in turn derived from 'pytho', *python.* The Greek understanding was that Python was potent even after it had died: it left behind a spiritual stench that infected people with jealousy.

Threshold spirits still have a trap to spring even after we've overcome them. Make no mistake, their strategy is such that even their death will aid their cause. It's not unlike the spiritual principle that the blood of the martyrs is the seed of the church.

This is why it's so important to keep hold of God's hand all the time. Even after you've crossed the threshold, there are dangers. As you overcome Python, it's wise to ask the Holy Spirit to blow away the stench of jealousy before it can reach any of your friends, family or acquaintances.

It's easy to see why Jonathan would have been envious of his cousin. Hailed as a hero for his self-sacrificing courage, acclaimed for stopping the plague, protected by God Himself from the full application of the Law for murder, Phinehas basked in an unconditional covenant and God's approving smile.

Meantime the family of Moses had slipped into such obscurity that we know absolutely nothing about the life of Gershom. It must have been galling for Jonathan to see the descendants of his grandfather's brother, Aaron, lauded and applauded while his own family became relative nobodies. Every feast day Eleazar, then later Phinehas, would have been on stage before the people, wearing a jewelled ephod reserved for the high priest. No wonder Jonathan wanted one of his own. No wonder he was tempted by Micah's offer.

It's my theory that envy constitutes a spiritual passageway of defilement. As far as generational streams go, it should have been Aaron's line through Phinehas that struggled with idolatry involving golden calves. But it isn't. It's the line of Moses, through Jonathan. I believe that particular spiritual issue passed from one generational stream to another through the medium of envy.

Nearly all men can stand adversity, but if you want to test a man's character, give him power.

Abraham Lincoln

Jonathan and Phinehas were meant to be close allies, to work together to enhance the amphictyonic league their grandfathers created in the twelve tribes. The similarity in the meaning of their names tells us that. They were unfortunately rivals. But under-rated as both of them are today, it means that most Christians have never realised Jonathan was responsible for destroying the tribal unity his grandfather worked so hard to build. Nor do they know that the early Christians considered his journey to Gibeah to be intimately linked with that of Jesus to Emmaus.

In addition, most of us have never heard of the very specialised, peculiar position Phinehas held within the Levitical priesthood and, as a consequence, have never realised the significance of some very peculiar actions of Jesus. Phinehas was considered to be the first 'war messiah'.

At the time of Jesus, the Jewish people were expecting not one, but two, messiahs. One was the 'Son of David' who was expected to come to rule as a king and sit on the throne of David. The war messiah, on the other hand, was prophesied to be the 'Son of Joseph'; he was expected to die in combat with the enemies of God and of Israel.

Now by 'Son of Joseph', it was commonly understood that this messiah would come from the tribe of Ephraim, the second son of the patriarch Joseph.

These two messiahs were considered to be members of the 'Four Craftsmen' mentioned in Zechariah 1:20. These Four Craftsmen were popularly understood to be Elijah; the Son of David; the Son of Joseph; the Righteous Priest.

Elijah was believed to be a prophet who would herald the coming of the two messiahs. Jesus Himself identified 'Elijah' as John the Baptist (Matthew 17:12); but it's doubtful any of His disciples thought He combined the other three Craftsmen in His person. I wonder which messiah Simon thought Jesus was when, at Caesarea Philippi, he identified Jesus as *'the Messiah, the Son of the living God.'* Was Simon thinking of the kingly messiah or the war messiah?

Suddenly the emphases of the different gospels become clear. Matthew, Mark and, to a lesser extent, Luke proclaim the kingly messiah, the 'Son of David'. The book of Hebrews in proclaiming Jesus as a priest after the order of Melchizedek, *righteous king*, has its focus on a type of priestly messiah. But it's John who repeatedly and uniquely uses the term, 'Son of Joseph'. We've missed the fact he was announcing Jesus as the war messiah, the successor to Phinehas. Jesus was the fulfilment of the prophecies encoded in the peculiar words and letters of Numbers 25. He was the broken Word who was also the harbinger of the covenant of peace wrought by a hand with a spear.

The war messiah was the priest anointed for war[91] who led out the Ark of the Covenant in advance of the armies of Israel, praising and worshipping God all the while. To fulfil that aspect of prophecy, Jesus had to be a war leader. Perhaps that why this curious interchange takes place, straight after He tells Peter he will deny Him three times: *Then Jesus asked them, 'When I sent you without purse, bag or sandals, did you lack anything?' 'Nothing,' they answered. He said to them, 'But now if you have a purse, take it, and also a bag; and if you don't have a sword, sell your cloak and buy one. It is written: "And he was numbered with the transgressors"; and I tell you that this must be fulfilled in Me. Yes, what is written about Me is reaching its fulfilment.' The disciples said, 'See, Lord, here are two swords.' 'That's enough!' He replied.* (Luke 22:35-38 NIV)

Jewish tradition names the two spies who went to Jericho as Caleb and Phinehas. Christians are more apt to surmise that one of them was Salmon, a prince of Judah, since he married Rahab and was the father of Boaz. There's plenty of controversy over the identity of Rahab—is she or is she not the inn-keeper and perhaps prostitute of Jericho?

Given the rarity of women's names in Scripture, I'm inclined to think it is the same woman. For two reasons: first, there's no real point in mentioning her name unless they were the same person—confusion would arise where recognition is meant to be accorded; and secondly, it explains why Boaz was so accommodating to the foreigner Ruth. His mother was also a foreigner.

However, if it's true that Phinehas was the second spy, then yet again, he is involved in a significant threshold covenant episode.

Even more significantly, he is involved with Rahab who is generally considered to have been a prostitute. This incident is then a complete reversal of what happens in the Valley of Acacias. There, Phinehas was responsible for the killing of a ritual prostitute and her lover. Here he had his life saved by one. And because of a threshold covenant, no less!

There are such fine mirror aspects to the stories that I'm more inclined to believe Phinehas was the second spy than that he wasn't. From heaven's point of view, he needs another threshold test with different nuances. From an earthly point of view, Joshua needs to send in spies to Jericho who have demonstrated a lack of fear in threshold tests. Who, faced with Python, Rachab and Leviathan, have stood their ground and not yielded.

Caleb is an obvious choice, despite his age. He'd have been in his late seventies. The other obvious choice is Joshua himself, but he's on the threshold of receiving the mantle of leadership from Moses.

Phinehas is, in fact, the next logical choice.

Because he was apparently the only member of the assembly whose reaction at a threshold had been tried and tested and not found wanting. To send anyone else would be to risk a repeat of the twelve-spies episode and another forty years in the desert.

In *Shadows of the Shoah*, an immersive presentation about the Holocaust, one of the survivors of Auschwitz spoke of witnessing an awkward moment between two sisters. Kitia described one of them wrenching a blanket away from the other with the words, 'I must survive.'

She reflected: 'Auschwitz didn't change people. It revealed what was deep inside.'

At moments of trauma, in harrowing times and circumstances, the truth about each individual human nature is revealed. Humanity is capable of behaviour so vile and monstrous, it is beyond all comprehension. We are also capable of nobility and self-sacrificial love so honourable that it's equally beyond comprehension.

In Scripture, it's easy to spot the threshold moments orchestrated by God. At least one angel and sometimes hosts of them are in attendance. The armies of the Lord of heaven are on battle-alert at these moments. If we can be struck down at this point so we never achieve our destiny, it'll be a coup for the forces of hell. More importantly, all the effort heaven has put into bringing us to that point will be wasted.

A threshold is the perfect moment for the Enemy to strike to inflict maximum damage on God's plans towards us for good and not for harm. And instinctively, without ever being told of the spiritual dynamic involved, we just know that thresholds require a sacrifice. And when, suddenly and terrifyingly, Python and Rachab appear, demanding an offering, what choice will we make?

Who will we sacrifice? Others? Ourselves? God?

Until that unique moment we step up to a threshold, that's truly an unanswerable question. We don't know what's hidden deep inside ourselves or inside others until we observe the sacrifice on the final step across a threshold.

Just as Auschwitz didn't change people, thresholds don't either. But they do reveal what's deep inside.

What was deep inside Phinehas was zeal for the holiness of God shot through with self-sacrifice and compassion for his community. And God honoured it in his clash with Baal Peor, the constricting spirit of Python.

But how would the zeal of Phinehas fare if he were to confront Rachab, the spirit of wasting? Indeed, the spirit of wasting is the logical opponent for Phinehas at this point: it's the one that wants to set at naught all he's achieved to this point.

So it's no coincidence that the person the two spies encounter in Jericho is the inn-keeper Rahab, named for another threshold spirit—another monster of the deep.

The initial sense of freedom when we are released from the squeeze of Python into the spaciousness of Rachab is a mark of the subtlety of the deception. Python tries to constrict our circumstances; to make them tight, narrow, restricted. Rachab on the other hand tries to broaden our circumstances; to make them wide, open, unrestricted.

Although these threshold spirits sound like they're opposites, they work very well as allies and their agenda is the same. To stop us crossing the threshold. To get us to sacrifice to them and reaffirm the covenants of our forefathers. To block us from coming into our destiny and calling.

Rachab's name means *broad. Spread out. Wide*. This spirit wants to undermine our achievements, to spread us so thin across so many different activities that we're exhausted and not doing any of them as well as we could.

None of these activities need be bad in themselves—they can be good, even great. But they won't be your calling. This spirit wants to drain you; to get you to invest time, money, emotion, energy and effort into wasteful choices.

It's a spirit of wasting. It's a spirit that tempts us to 'do nothing' while assuring us we're simply waiting on God to open the right door.

It's also a spirit of arrogance and anger.

Some lexicons translate its name as *proud* or *storm*; JB Phillips in his translation[92] of Isaiah 30:7 brilliantly describes it as 'the Spent Whirlwind'. This alludes to the wheeling nature of the cherubim, an angelic class to which Rachab once belonged, but also declares it to be a washed-up, worn-out force.

The two spies sent into Jericho had a very different kind of challenge to that of Python. Caleb, traditionally the older of the spies, had been to the Promised Land before and had encountered the Python spirit operating through the giants of Hebron. These descendants of the Nephilim were sons of Anak, *the strangler, the choker*.

The spirit of wasting is a different proposition, however.

It doesn't try to choke us. Instead it tries to puff us up. What it latches onto in people is pride—even when that pride is disguised as shame.

Pride is the hook that Rachab used to snare Rehoboam, son of Solomon. Rehoboam has 'rachab' embedded in his name, which no doubt was intended to mean *broaden the kingdom*. Such a name was supposed to be prophetic of the extension of Solomon's realm to even greater and more glorious heights. But the arrogance and pride of Rachab were also there and the wise choice for Rehoboam would have been to turn his back on that aspect of his name. But he didn't and that was his undoing. He didn't listen to older and wiser heads and, as a result, he was left with a divided kingdom and a tiny remnant of land to rule.

By utilising pride, Rachab can bring about its agenda of wasting.

Now zeal and pride tend to go together. So it could be expected that Phinehas would have come to his downfall in Jericho. Especially when he found himself in the house of a prostitute. In covenant with her. He'd killed a man of the tribe of Simeon for covenanting with a prostitute, after all.

But pride doesn't seem to have been part of the nature of Phinehas or Caleb. Rabbinic tradition relates that they entered Jericho disguised as pot-sellers. 'Here are pots! Here are pots!' they cried. These words reveal their essential attitude of humility. They saw themselves primarily as vessels for the will of God.

'An earthenware pot's only value is the ability to hold something,' says Rabbi Yechiel Eckstein in commenting on this tradition. 'These men placed no value on their own egos. Rather, they saw their only value as serving as vessels for the will of God. The result was that they succeeded where others had failed.'[93]

Psalm 106:30 NIV tells us a little more about the character of Phinehas: *'But Phinehas stood up and intervened, and the plague was checked.'*

The King James Bible translates the same verse: *'Then stood up Phinehas, and executed judgment: and so the plague was stayed.'*

The Aramaic Bible in Plain English renders this: *'Phinehas stood up and prayed and the plague was restrained.'*

The God's Word Translation suggests: *'Then Phinehas stood between God and the people, and the plague was stopped.'*

All these differing translations have much to recommend them. At the heart of their varying nuances—*intervened*; *executed judgment*; *prayed*; *stood between God and the people*—is the Hebrew word 'palal', meaning both *judge* and *pray*.

Not words we're used to considering as intimately related.

We are called to judge angels.

'Do you not know that the saints will judge the world?... Do you not know that we will judge angels?' (1 Corinthians 6:2–3 NIV)

Herein lies the nub of what the threshold is all about. Why the opposition is so fierce, so prolonged, so unremitting.

When you are able to go in and out across that threshold, when you can move freely back and forward, when you have the keys of authority to lock or unlock the doors at will, then you are qualified to *sit* in the gateway. And that is the ancient image of a judge: one who sits at the gate.

Yes, crossing the threshold means you are well on the way to judging the very angelic beings who have been bent on your destruction.

And they know this.

So they don't even want you to get to first base. They've got back-up plans upon back-up plans. The spirits of forgetting, constriction, wasting, backlash, rejection, vampire and legion in one sense see you as being as insignificant as an ant. However, in another sense, they can't afford to be contemptuous of you because you are potentially a supreme threat. *You*—a disgusting little worm in their sight, a repulsive hybrid of spirit and clayey body—are going to judge *them*!

Yes, *judge*.

It's no coincidence that we've been convinced by our modern Christian culture that Jesus prohibited judging others. *'Do not judge, or you too will be judged,'* says the New International's translation of Matthew 7:1, reflecting a standard across-the-board interpretation in various English versions.

Al Houghton makes the point that, if someone told us not to pray, we'd be downright suspicious about their theology. But few of us are suspicious when we are told not to judge. Yet, as he points out,[94] the exhortation in Matthew 7:1 is part of a sequence:

Don't pray... as the hypocrites do. (Matthew 6:5 and following)
Don't give... as the hypocrites do. (Matthew 6:2 and following)
Don't fast... as the hypocrites do. (Matthew 6:16 and following)

Don't judge... as the hypocrites do. (Matthew 7:1 and following)

Without this understanding of context, Jesus contradicts Himself within a single sentence where He informs us how justice operates. *'For in the same way you judge others, you will be judged, and with the measure you use, it will be measured to you.'* (Matthew 7:2 NIV)

In other words, if you are hypocritical about the way you judge, you will be swallowed up by your own verdicts.

On the threshold, we have to be able to stand in the judgments we call down.

Like Phinehas, we have to be able to call down saving judgment from heaven. And like Phinehas, we have to be able to stand in that judgment.

Rabbinic tradition relates that Phinehas did not want to carry out his act of judgment alone—he was concerned, amongst other things, that he'd be killed by a lynch mob. He recognised that he could not ask anyone from the tribe of Reuben to help—because Reuben had lost his place as the firstborn, generations previously, due to sexual sin. Nor could he ask anyone from the tribe of Simeon—for that was where the present sin was being committed, at the highest levels.

He asked the Levites but got no takers. Even Moses was silent, unsure what to do.

Now the amazing thing about Phinehas is that he didn't rely on a formula. He recognises that it's a relationship with God that is the critical issue. Rahab might be a pagan prostitute but her nascent faith, as exemplified in her covenant-keeping, is all that really matters when it comes to judging her case. Zimri, on the other hand, might have been a prince of Israel but his unfaithfulness to the Law and his covenant-breaking is all that really mattered when it came to judging his.

Jesus, as the 'war messiah', is the Judge of all the earth.

On the day of Pentecost, Peter preached: *'Let all the house of Israel therefore know for certain that God has made Him both Lord and Christ, this Jesus whom you crucified.'* (Acts 2:36 ESV)

Lord and Christ. In other words:

Christ: kingly messiah—God's anointed ruler.
Lord: war messiah—God's appointed judge.

We conflate 'Lord' and 'Christ' in our thinking, merging them into one; yet they have completely different nuances.

In the Courts of Heaven, the royal court and the judicial court are separate places. Many Christians have become attuned to operating in the Courts but don't have ease of movement between them or within them, or have an ability to pass into the chambers of the Divine Council.

What is the difference?

In the judicial court are the accused, the plaintiffs and the judges. We can take any of these roles, yet it is God's desire for us to learn to sit at His gate as the judges.

In the royal court are ambassadors, witnesses and worshippers. Again we can take any of these roles and should be taking all of them.

In the Divine Council are prophets, negotiators and strategists. Here God consults with His creation about the best way to achieve His purposes. Now is the moment to do several things: pick your jaw up off the floor and dismiss the thought that you couldn't possibly have read that last sentence correctly.

Yes, it's true. God is not a dictator. Consider the revelation of Micaiah about the discussion in the courts of heaven over the best method to lure Ahab to his death (1 Kings 22). Micaiah's knowledge of God's counsel and His strategic plans is in accord with the words of Amos: *'Surely the Sovereign Lord does nothing without revealing His plan to His servants the prophets.'* (Amos 3:7 NIV) It is also in accord with the revelation of Ezekiel 13:9 that false prophets are not in the Council of God's people.

God's appointed prophets, however, don't seem to think twice about negotiating with Him. Straight after Abraham made a threshold covenant with God, he began to negotiate over the fate of Sodom. In the midst of wrestling a name covenant from God, Jacob negotiated for a blessing. Joshua had just recovered from re-affirming the covenant between God and His people[95] when the Commander of the Lord's

Hosts appeared and he opened a negotiation with him.

Ratification of a threshold covenant does seem to be the moment when permission is granted for a person to become a negotiator. For example, Mary, mother of Jesus, negotiated with Him at His own threshold event: the first miracle at the wedding feast of Cana. After Jesus undertakes a threshold covenant on behalf of the church at the Transfiguration, He sent seventy of His disciples out in pairs. In doing so, He was clearly making an earthly copy of the heavenly Council which has seventy members.

In the courts of heaven, God consults, hears and heeds pleas, changes His mind on the basis of prayers and appeals, declares the conditions for reversing a decision. Somehow, we've become convinced that God is a king in the manner of the Medes and the Persians—He issues a fiat and it can never be overturned.

It's true there are some issues on which He will not budge. But there are plenty of times, as Scripture testifies, that He is willing to shift position: Amos negotiated with Him about the fate of Israel (Amos 7); Ezekiel negotiated about the kind of dung he could use for cooking fuel (Ezekiel 4); Abimelech negotiated over his death sentence (Genesis 20); so did Hezekiah (2 Kings 20); Moses negotiated over God's proposal to abandon the idolatrous Israelites and start over (Exodus 32); Habakkuk negotiated about the apparent lack of a divine answer to his complaint (Habakkuk 1); the Syro-Phoenician woman who wanted just the crumbs that fell from the Master's table negotiated for her daughter (Matthew 15) and Simon Peter negotiated Jesus down from 'agápē', *sacrificial love*, to 'phileo', *friendship* (John 21).

An earthly king might fear to lose his authority; might worry he'd be seen as weak or vacillating if he changes his mind. But God *is* authority; as the Author and Perfecter of our faith, He doesn't need to worry about anyone's perception of Him. When God 'changes His mind', it's not about making a mistake. It's about friendship. It's about valuing His relationship with us more than He values His own dignity. Such honour is beyond comprehension.

Psalm 82 is a short song many people try not to think too deeply about, lest it wreck their theological preconceptions about heaven.

God has taken His place in the divine council;
in the midst of the gods He holds judgment:
'How long will you judge unjustly
and show partiality to the wicked?' Selah
'Give justice to the weak and the fatherless;
maintain the right of the afflicted and the destitute.
Rescue the weak and the needy;
deliver them from the hand of the wicked.'

They have neither knowledge nor understanding,
they walk about in darkness;
all the foundations of the earth are shaken.

I said, 'You are gods,
sons of the Most High, all of you;
nevertheless, like men you shall die,
and fall like any prince.'

Arise, O God, judge the earth;
for You shall inherit all the nations!

Psalm 82:1-8 ESV

Who are these 'gods'(!) in God's Council? Some translators have such obvious misgivings they use 'rulers' instead of 'gods', making it clear they believe the verse is meant to refer to human beings. But Jesus quotes this psalm in a way that I believe precludes this interpretation. When the Jewish leaders picked up stones to kill Him,

Jesus answered them, "Is it not written in your Law, 'I said, you are gods'? If He called them gods to whom the word of God came—and Scripture cannot

be broken—do you say of Him whom the Father consecrated and sent into the world, 'You are blaspheming,' because I said, 'I am the Son of God'?

John 10:34-36 ESV

Jesus is defending His claim to be God in this passage. It doesn't make sense to suggest He is using verse 6 of the psalm in the belief it refers to human princes or to mortal judges. His argument would then be pointless. Perhaps verse 7 of the psalm with its theme, 'you're gonna die,' could be a rhetorical, redundant point to remind human beings of their transience. However, it makes much more sense as an explosive final verdict on angelic opposition to God's rule. They've sowed death: they'll reap it. It's a warning to them not to be too cocksure about their status as immortal beings.

It's my belief that Jesus fulfilled the prophecy of the opening line—*God has taken His place in the divine council*—at the Transfiguration. As I've previously indicated, I believe His appearance in glory occurred on Mount Hermon in northern Israel. To make His stand in the Divine Council, Jesus had to climb the 'mount of assembly' to challenge the 'gods'. He had to ascend to the residence of the Canaanite gods, appear in their midst and denounce their partiality to the wicked, their refusal to preside over justice and thus their coming downfall.

Mount Hermon was considered to be the site of the palace of the Canaanite pantheon.[96] It's no coincidence that, just six days prior to this at Caesarea Philippi, Jesus said to Simon Peter: '*...on this rock I will build my church, and the gates of hell shall not prevail against it.*'

There was a cave called the 'Gates of Hell' at Caesarea Philippi, below Mount Hermon. Human sacrifice was sometimes practised there at the Temple of Pan. This location was also not far from the sanctuary at Dan where the descendants of Jonathan the Levite set up worship of a golden calf.

But the 'gates of hell' is also an oblique way of saying 'demonic judges'. Because in ancient times, judges sat in the gates, the two words become synonymous. So Jesus was declaring that the church would not be subject to the judgments of fallen angels with their destructive and unjust proclamations. As Paul pointed out in 1 Corinthians 6:3, it would be exactly the reverse.

It was during a name covenant that Jesus gave this blessing to the church. He and Simon exchanged names: Simon called Jesus 'messiah' and Jesus called him 'Peter'.

Now a name covenant requires 'implantation' through a threshold covenant six days later. And this is what Jesus did by going up the 'mount of assembly'; He undertook a threshold covenant with Peter, James and John as representatives of the future church and, in doing so, He confirmed His word that the rule of the demonic judges was over.

Coming down the mountain, He backed up His sentencing of these dark powers by creating an earthly copy of the Divine Council. He sent out seventy disciples[97] who, when they return, rejoiced that even the demons obeyed them at the use of Jesus' name. (Luke 10:17)

Jesus replied, '*I saw Satan fall like lightning from heaven...*' (Luke 10:18 BSB)

This fulfilled the prophecy of Psalm 82:7 that the 'gods' would fall from the heavenly Council. Along with the fall, the shaking of the earth was prophesied. Which makes me wonder whether the reverse is true: if an earthquake occurs, is this a sign of the overthrow of principalities and powers?

I'm inclined to think there may be a connection. Although the Hebrew term in Psalm 82 for *shake* is 'mot',[98] a cognate word is 'palats', *tremble*, which is related to 'pallatsuth', *shuddering*. These may in turn be related[99] to 'palal', *judge, pray, intercede, entreat* through 'palat', *deliver* or *escape*—since a judge's verdict can be a means of deliverance.

All these various elements—prayer, intercession, judgment, earthquake, deliverance—combine in a single story shot through with threshold covenant overtones. Paul and Silas were in prison at Philippi, having been thrown there by the local justices because they'd caused trouble by delivering a slave girl of a Python spirit. At midnight while they were praying and singing hymns, an earthquake occurred. All the prison doors flew open and the prisoners' chains fell off. The jailer, sure that everyone had escaped, was about to kill himself when Paul calls out to him. 'What must I do to be saved?' the jailer asks—rounding off a story which began with the deliverance of a slave girl and finishes with the deliverance of an entire family.

And, in case you didn't notice, let me point out the name covenant in governance over these circumstances. God, the divine poet, is drawing forth 'palats', 'palal' and 'palat' from the name Paul.

So how do we become the sort of righteous judges who can bring saving justice to the earth? Bearing in mind the possibility that summoning justice down from heaven may be earth-shaking—in the most literal possible way.

Some people might back away at this point, thinking: 'I don't want to rock the boat, shake the earth or cause problems.'

But—the longer injustice prevails, the greater the eventual shaking.

There's no escaping the issue. We can't pray for universal peace or a world without shaking—God will not answer those prayers because they ask Him to negate His own word: *'You will hear of wars and rumours of wars... Nation will rise against nation, and kingdom against kingdom. There will be famines and earthquakes in various places.'* (Matthew 24:6–7 NIV)

Still we can ask for such matters to be minimised. We can negotiate on behalf of our world. Intercessory prayer brings judgment. Such verdicts may deliver friends, family, communities, cities, nations from injustice, greed and malice. Such injustice, greed and malice may be within or without. And that's the judgment aspect of it: if we pray for justice in a situation, those we are praying for have to be able to stand in that justice. Because the measure that we mete out is the measure that will be meted to us.

We have to be able to stand in the fire we call down.

We have to have the zeal of Phinehas for the holiness of God and also his willingness to risk entering the curse. We have to be like Esther, born for such a time as this, and ready to say, *'If I perish, I perish.'*

(Esther 4:16 NIV)

We have to be able to pass those tests we failed previously or that generations before us have consistently failed. By trusting God and remaining faithful to Jesus, we the church demonstrate the mystery of His grace to the principalities and powers. It is through us that God's redemptive wisdom is made known to the angels. It is through us that God chooses to judge both the world and the angel hosts.

The responsibility is enormous.

The authority is staggering.

And the empowering grace is continually available.

7

Judging Angels

I'M REGULARLY INVOLVED IN PRAYER MINISTRY—like other people who volunteer in this area, I help people in crisis to look at the present unmanageability of their lives in terms of root causes from the past. Although my speciality is guiding others through the unravelling of ungodly threshold covenants, that's not the place to start. In fact, it's getting towards the end of the journey.

Discerning prayer ministers will sniff out condemnatory beliefs about the way the world works; they'll rootle around looking for evidence of internal vows made in childhood; they'll seek out sinful reactions from the past still haunting the present. They're looking for patterns. And so they are performing a prophetic work. The Greeks may have understood prophecy as foretelling but the Hebrews understood it as forth-telling. In Scripture, prophecy was about the proclamation of pattern. Whether it was in number, in name, in time, season or circumstance, prophecy was about discerning the principles of God's design and applying them to a given situation.

Prayer ministry is not just a prophetic work. It's a huge responsibility because, when someone trusts me with their story and asks me to come with them and Jesus into a prayer space, I'm effectively sitting in judgment on their lives.

I'm not sure I understood the depths of this until, one night, I had a dream about walking a corridor of heaven and being accosted by two angels. 'Just the person we wanted to see,' one said as he grabbed me by the arm. 'Quickly, come and judge this case.'

'I can't possibly do that!' I protested as they hustled me into a courtroom and escorted me to a judge's bench.

The moment I sat down all extra-sensory perception was gone. By 'extra-sensory perception', I mean I was instantly stripped of all ability to recognise the meaning and significance of voice level, facial expression, body language or accent. All the subtle clues that come from different postures and gestures, cadences and inflections of tone, the carriage of a person, the emotional aura they exude—gone. In a flash. I hadn't been aware how much I used these skills until they were flattened into non-existence.

A man was brought into the courtroom.

Later, when my 'extra-sensory perception' returned, I realised he was both furious and horrified. His worst nightmare had come to pass. He was about to be judged by... a *woman*.

Fortunately I didn't have to open the case because he announced, 'I shouldn't be here. I can say, "Jesus is Lord."'

This isn't so hard, I thought to myself, within the dream. *All that's needed is a simple check.* 'That's fantastic. I just need to clarify one point. This "Jesus" you say is Lord, could you be a bit more specific? Perhaps you could say "Jesus of Nazareth is Lord" just so we can be sure it's the same Jesus that we're talking about.'

'Yes, I can do that.'

If my other senses were on-line, I'd have recognised the scorn and hostility edging the man's voice. I'd have registered the ramrod stiffness of his back and the barely concealed scowl. But when you've got flat-line words and you've lost the ability to detect any add-ons, that's what you go with: words, and words alone.

I waited for the man to get around to doing what he said he could, but he was silent.

'So,' I said, 'can you please repeat your statement about Jesus being Lord and add something to identify the Jesus you're referring to.'

'I told you I could do that.'

'It doesn't have to be "of Nazareth", if you think that's not specific enough. You could pick something from one of the Creeds—'suffered under Pontius Pilate'; 'born of the virgin Mary'. If you don't think Mary was a virgin, pick something else. We're not saved by doctrine, but by grace through faith. My preference would be for some statement about the resurrection, but it can be whatever you like.'

'Yes, of course, I can say any of that.'

I waited.

Silence.

'Maybe I've haven't explained the problem here very well. There are counterfeiting spirits who call themselves "Jesus". So I just like to be clear which Jesus you have a relationship with and who is your lord.'

'But I've told you.'

'You've told me you can say any of the statements I've suggested but you haven't actually made a declaration out loud of any of them. Perhaps you *can* but you haven't.' I stopped and stared into his eyes. 'And the truth is that, if I asked you to repeat word-for-word after me, "Jesus of Nazareth is Lord," you couldn't actually do it, could you?'

I watched the man's face crumble in sudden horror as he realised the truth. At that moment, all those senses I'd been stripped of flooded back in an instant. I recognised his accent, knew his nationality, grasped the confused anger and passive aggression behind his demeanour.

The angels took hold of him.

And I woke up.

As I analysed the extraordinarily vivid memory of the dream, I knew that I'd been tested—I hadn't judged the case; I had simply led the man to judge himself.

And this is what prayer ministry should be: leading a person to see they are being judged in the same way that they have judged others.

Many Christians believe in the primacy of the blood of Jesus—that is, they believe that the blood of Jesus has washed them clean of all sin and, as a consequence, God will not hold them to account for violating His Word.

Let's put this another way and ask the question: does the covering of the blood of Jesus give us the authority to violate the word of God?

Let's examine a common scenario: a Christian leader takes a group of followers on a mission trip in a South-east Asian country and, because the opportunity presents itself, they enter a temple to curse Buddha. This is in violation of God's Word as given in Jude 1:9-10 and 2 Peter 2:10-11 where the consequences of such activity are spelled out in considerable detail.

When we use the blood of Jesus as a covering to violate God's word, we are practising witchcraft. The whole purpose of witchcraft is to use God's creative design—the physical laws He has embedded in nature and the enormous power of the spoken words delivered with intent—against His rule.

Ignorance is no excuse. Whenever we use God's Word as an activation principle to bring about results to satisfy our own goals, rather than the expansion of His kingdom, we are operating in magic.

Not faith.

The practice of magic is deeply embedded in today's church. Its natural partner since the time of Pythagoras, some five hundred years before the birth of Christ, is logic. Throughout the centuries, the most consistent opponent of Christianity has been Pythagorean philosophy. Today, we see it split into two fronts: science on one hand and new age religion on the other.

We're so enamoured with logic, we don't realise its insidious influence on the interpretation of God's Word. For example, many people believe that, because 'it's all done at the Cross', it is unnecessary to confess sin because God has already completely forgiven those who've turned to Him. This is in violation of 1 John 1:9 and James 5:16,[100] and so they have to be explained away.

To interpret Scripture through the theological filter of 'it's all done at the Cross', rather than to understand what 'it's all done at the Cross' means through the lens of Scripture, is to manipulate God's Word. It's not only to follow the example of the satan but, in many cases, it's to elevate logic to the position of final arbiter on the Word of God.

God is not illogical but neither can He be explained by pure logic. Logic is a human invention; He transcends it.

Logic is designed to demonstrate truth by systematic argument. It has limitations. If a pair of assumptions leads to a contradiction or a logical paradox, then one or both of the assumptions is declared to be false. If we turn logic loose on trying to understand God's nature, we'd quickly conclude He can be just or He can be merciful, but not both. They are contradictory qualities: perfect justice is incompatible with mercy; perfect mercy is incompatible with justice.

Greek thinking, dominated by logic, leads many Christians to try to resolve Scriptural paradoxes by creating hierarchies: the writings of Paul first, the words of Jesus next, the epistles of John a fair bit further down, while James—the letter Martin Luther called the 'epistle of straw'—rates towards the bottom. Slipped entirely off the ladder, floating somewhere around in outer darkness, are the epistles of Peter and Jude.

Is it a surprise to realise that Paul rates above Jesus?

It shouldn't be. Jesus is frequently conditional, Paul *appears* to be unconditional.

Jesus says, '*Forgive others and you will be forgiven,*' (Luke 6:37 NIV) while Paul unilaterally says, '*In Him, we have... forgiveness of sins.*' (Ephesians 1:7 NIV)

Those who rate Paul's writings above the words of Jesus justify their position by an appeal to chronology: Paul wrote after the resurrection while Jesus spoke prior to it. The human heart wants to believe that Paul means that God's unmerited favour covers sin so automatically that it is hidden away instantly so God sees nothing.

Yet English has more than one meaning for *cover*. Theologically, a slippage seems to have occurred over the last few centuries from one meaning to another. Insurance companies still use *cover* in the sense of offering funds to repair all the damage of an accident or disaster.

Is the blood of Jesus a *cover* in the sense of a concealment of sin? Or is it a *cover* in the sense of it being sufficient to restore, repair and bring back to a state of glory all that was ruined?

The Hebrew word for *cover* that also means *atone* comes from 'kaph', *threshold stone*. The blood of Jesus is the blood of the threshold covenant that atones for sin; that is, it brings us back into oneness with God and reconciles us to Him.

On Judgment Day, Jesus wants to present us as a surprise to His Father. As He was unrecognisable to Cleopas and Mary on the road to Emmaus, so He wants us to be just as unrecognisable to the Father. Any memory of what we were like in our sinful state will just be blown away by what we have become as a result of the power of His blood.

This is the triumph of Jesus: that He should be able to show us off as trophies of grace before the assembled host of heaven, shouting with delight, 'See what My blood has wrought!'

The wisdom of God and greatness of Jesus is that He can redeem every wasteful choice. He can restore the years the locusts have eaten; He can extend the time we need to defeat our enemies, just as He did for Joshua.

The covering of His blood isn't about hiding our tawdry, shameful sins under an impenetrable red veil. Heaven isn't going to applaud an invisible wreck. Instead it's about the blood of Jesus giving us the power to be transformed into a new creation that will cause gasps of 'Wow!' to echo across heaven. Thus Paul who could write, *'By grace you have been saved, through faith—and this is not from yourselves, it is the gift of God,'* (Ephesians 2:8 NIV) could also write without contradiction, *'Work out your own salvation with fear and trembling.'* (Philippians 2:12 KJV)

The emergence of the Bride should be met with stunned awe at what the blood of Jesus has accomplished as we have appropriated it into our lives.

We have to apply what God has supplied.

We're in partnership—*'We are God's co-workers.'* (1 Corinthians 3:9 GWT)

If we're going to come to that place that God wants for us where we act as His judges, we have to learn discernment. To recognise magic when we see it in operation, to detect when logic has reached the limits of its usefulness.

Many people are aware they've been called as a gatekeeper in God's kingdom. Part of the job profile involves protecting judges as well as, in some instances, being judges themselves.

It calls for an ability to differentiate between good and evil.

This is a tough call.

Because unsanctified mercy, unregenerate love, unhallowed justice, unconsecrated truth, ungodly peace can look exceptionally good on the surface. It's only when we bite into the fruit we discover it's diseased.

What does sin look like as a progressive process?

I have long been indebted to Ted Peters for his book, *Sin: Radical Evil in Soul and Society*.

As a younger Christian, I busily excused all those who offended me or committed sins against me in the mistaken belief that 'excusing' equalled 'forgiving'. If there had been an Olympic event for unsanctified mercy, I'd have been a gold medal contender. When God pointed out my sin during the writing of *Merlin's Wood*, I realised that I'd have to learn to judge others, in order to forgive them. 'If I'm going to judge angels one day,' I said to myself, 'I'd better start to learn how to get this right.'

Latterly I've realised that judgment is not only a necessary precursor to true forgiveness, it's also a necessary precursor to true peace. Phinehas shows us this in the Valley of Acacias. It is through his willingness to bring judgment and stand under the same judgment that a covenant of peace was given to him and his descendants forever.

Ted Peters' book was invaluable in helping me re-wire my thinking so that my natural inclination to excuse others, rationalise their behaviour, tolerate their conduct—however sinful, hypocritical or unjust—was brought into deeper alignment with God's values.

I'm still learning.

Peters' book is, in parts, not for the faint-hearted. There are some harrowing sections on ritual abuse. Nevertheless I still heartily recommend it, especially if you need a framework to stop your thinking defaulting back to unsanctified mercy or unregenerate love. And if, as a result of those unredeemed patterns of thought, you're apt to become an enabler of sin in others.

Peters identified seven stages in the descent into 'evil'. As he points out, they may not come in this particular order; sometimes they seem to arrive all at once. Nevertheless it's helpful to use this chronology.

He begins with ANXIETY. This, while not in any way evil in itself, readies us for choices that are inappropriate.

Second, he lists a word he coined himself: 'UNFAITH'. Going beyond doubt or lack of faith, this is a loss of trust sufficiently catastrophic to cause the person to decide to rely only on themselves, to never be vulnerable and to never give their heart to another.

This naturally leads to the third stage: PRIDE.

Fourthly comes CONCUPISCENCE. Although this word is usually associated with sexual lust, it is simply an insatiable drive to control another person. It's a desire to bend other people to your will; to enslave them.

The fifth stage is SELF-JUSTIFICATION which almost inevitably involves the regular scape-goating of another person.

The sixth is CRUELTY.

And the last is BLASPHEMY.

Now this kind of blasphemy isn't the casual swearing of a male locker room.[101]

The kind of blasphemy Ted Peters considers is different by several orders of magnitude: it's pre-meditated, malevolent and invariably involves symbol reversal.

When the conscience is so completely seared that 'good' and 'evil' are inverted; when sanctified symbols are presented as perverted and unholy, we reach a terminus. This kind of blasphemy enthrones wickedness. No pity exists, no trace of self-loathing for the harm done or the trauma caused. Cruelty at this unimaginable level strives to ensure that the victim of abuse will *never* ever be able to receive spiritual comfort. When victims are traumatised through harrowing experience to not just believe but to know that love equals murder, the 'sin against the Holy Spirit' is in operation.

Jesus clearly speaks of this—the unforgivable sin—in the context of inverted good and evil and, in so doing, withdrawing all divine comfort from those who need healing. (Mark 3:22–30) Victims are programmed by the blasphemers so the name of Jesus is synonymous with unspeakable terror; baptism with death by drowning.

Peters suggests that evil begins at stage two, unfaith. Personally, I like to think it emerges at stage seven. However, I also think that defining the stage at which evil begins is not nearly as important as being able to identify its hallmarks. When I can spot its distinguishing marks, this stops me in my tracks when I hear the casually flung propaganda of politicians. Or a man calling his ex-wife 'evil'. Or a woman describing her husband similarly.

Until all seven signifiers are there, I'm reluctant to label any situation 'evil'.

And helpful as I find these insights of Ted Peters, I'm far more interested in a related phenomenon.

Complicity with darkness.

Just why do 'nice people' decide to appease Python, Rachab and Leviathan by sacrificing others? And why do those other 'even nicer people' permit themselves to be sacrificed at the behest of these spirits?

Mostly, I believe, it's because we're complicit ourselves.

It's hard to recognise ourselves as enablers of sin in others. It's a crushing blow to our self-esteem.

At each stage, we become enablers of the other through our

unsanctified responses.

In our desire not to be lonely, we put our TRUST in those who have lost faith. And not in God.

In our desire to be liked, we become RETICENT, not speaking out as the proud make it clear they despise us for expressing a different viewpoint.

In our desire to appease and create peace with the proud as their drive to control becomes obsessive, we allow ourselves to be DISPOSSESSED.

In our desire to see a removal of the dispossession inflicted on our wider family or workplace, we became the SCAPEGOAT.

In our desire to see the good in our persecutors, we rationalise and excuse their behaviour, becoming TOLERANT.

In our desire to overcome blasphemy, we attempt to INVERT THE REVERSED SYMBOL others have created.

We need to be able to observe this entire ladder of enabling; a single episode of being robbed and dispossessed does not mean the whole scaffold is there.

But when we can see several of these attitudes within ourselves, we need to recognise that the problem is not simply the other person—it's also in ourselves. We have become complicit with sin by enabling it in others.

Once we've recognised the issue, the next step is to confess. It's wise to do this with both 1 John 1:9 and James 5:16 in mind. These verses show up a subtle distinction in the nature of confession: if we confess to God we are forgiven; if we confess to each other, we are healed.

In that confession, repent of the sin of enabling sin in others; renounce complicity with the spirits of the threshold.

Apply the death of Jesus on the cross to your habits of enabling, so that they brought to death.

Receive God's forgiveness and the release of His resurrection life.

Then live out the transformation.

What world-mending are you called to bring about? What restoration has God charged you with? The gospel is about God's *shalom*—His joy to the world, along with the advance of His kingdom of peace and mercy, justice and truth.

So how do you take that Good News to the world? You have been born in this era, this time, this generation, for a divine purpose. God has located you in a specific place, given you a particular family, friends and colleagues. All of them are there for a reason.

Who knows if—like Jesus on the road to Emmaus mending that terrible rupture that led to the tribal brotherhood turning like wolves upon each other—you are called to walk with a colleague and heal a generational conflict neither of you are aware of? Who knows if such immense repair is as simple as asking a stranger to dinner?

Before peace can come, judgment must. That's the lesson of Phinehas as he takes a spear to enter the curse as the plague raged amongst the Israelites.

Before forgiveness can occur, judgment must. Unless we can say, 'What you did was wrong,' without excusing, rationalising, justifying or absolving, we aren't in a position to add, '*But* I forgive you.' Instead we're trivialising the pain and offence with statements like: 'Well, she didn't know any better'; 'He wasn't brought up to know that's wounding'; 'He loves in his own way'; 'It didn't hurt that much anyway.'

Any proper understanding of judgment starts here: it is not in opposition to forgiveness but opens the way for it.

On 21 October 2016, a remarkable example of this occurred in the Mall in Washington D.C. A gathering of 1000 First Nation tribes from the USA and Canada convened a historic ceremony to forgive the US Government for all its broken treaties. Not every treaty is necessarily a covenant, but it's clear some of the ceremonies surrounding the signing of documents were covenantal in nature; thereby invoking blessings and curses. Every single treaty ever signed with the native

American tribes was broken.

These tribes recognised that the crises facing America and the suffering of so many dispossessed and disempowered people was partly a result of curses stemming from covenant violation. So they came together to proclaim forgiveness over the people of the United States, whether they wanted it or not. They wanted to see the festering poison that spiritually afflicted the whole 'body' of the nation drained away.

So they forgave.

But notice they also judged. They basically said: 'Every single treaty has been broken and the nation is reaping the consequences of covenant violation.' That's a right judgment. It's not an accusation. It's a statement of fact. It doesn't say: 'The government is evil.' So too, when we judge prior to forgiveness, we should avoid accusations and stick to the facts.

The primary coordinator of this demonstration of lavish love was Chief Negiel Bigpond.

On that same day, before I read of this ceremony, I was looking at the story of Phinehas where the Hebrew word, 'negeph', *plague*, from 'nagaph', *to strike* or *stumble,* occurs. This word 'nagaph' is used to describe the action of rejecting a covenant—that is, *striking, trampling* or *stumbling* on the threshold stone. I also happened to be checking out those words which have a head-rhyme with 'nagaph' like 'naga', *infection*, and 'nagan', *musician*.

And I saw the resonances with that unusual name, Negiel. First, I thought: with a name like that, I'll bet Chief Bigpond is an accomplished musician—and, of course, he is.

Secondly, I thought: Negiel's name covenant obviously encodes a destiny which involves choices around curses and covenants, national plagues and infection. Oh, and music. Anyone with the name Negiel is called to be like Phinehas: he has to be able to step into the curse, to judge the nation and, having done so, to stand in the fire he calls down from heaven.

Rick Joyner commented that one thousand tribes forgave the American government 'simply because they don't want us to suffer for wrongs done to them. Have you ever heard of anything so noble? How would our world change if we all started to think like that?'

And that is what God is calling each of us to. He wants us to pass the tests, to stand in the place of judgment as we call down judgment on ourselves and others.

He wants us to mend the world.

How do we do that?

We go with God.

And together we go make the song of our names into the poem of our calling.

To the thunderous, world-shaking glory of God.

Endnotes

1 As I grow older, I've discovered that those things that have remained a 'favourite' across many decades are invariably to do with some aspect of my own name. The words of *The Gypsy Rover*, as I learned them in my childhood, are about an anonymous young aristocrat who leaves her 'father's castle gate' and her 'fair young lover' to follow the gypsy rover. Little did I know until recent years that the ballad is based on a true story about a 'Lady Anne Hamilton'.

2 Genesis 22:1-19. Rabbi Jonathan Sacks in his debate with Richard Dawkins comments that we perceive this story through the lens of our own culture, which does not see in many parts of the Bible an extended polemic against power; in particular, the extended polemics against child sacrifice. This particular episode is one he said has been critically misunderstood. Dawkins describes it as 'child abuse' but Sacks points out that every self-respecting god at the time of Abraham demanded child sacrifice. Even the Romans understood the child to be the property of the parents and could be treated as such: an asset, a chattel, a possession. The whole test was therefore to imprint on Abraham's mind and that of his descendants forever that children belong to God and that parents are guardians, they are not owners.

3 There is no general agreement on what the ten tests are. However, even Chuck Pierce in *A Time to Triumph: How to Win the War Ahead* (Chosen Books, 2016) maintains that Abraham passed several tests which include these same ones in Egypt and Gerar. It is my view, however, he failed the first so badly God had him redo it. Whereupon he failed again.

4 The Hebrew word for *silver* is 'keseph' and, from it, names like Casper, *treasury*, are derived. This links it to Zaphenath-Paaneah, *treasury of the glorious rest*, the name Pharaoh gave Joseph, son of Jacob. The syllable 'zaph' is obviously a pun on 'seph', the second syllable of Joseph. Removing the 'Jo' deletes the name of God, leaving just the idea of *adding* or *accumulating*.

5 Now, while there is no mention of the length of time in Scripture between the name covenant and the threshold covenant El Shaddai made with Abraham, traditionally it is said to be three days. Christian scholars follow rabbinic commentary in this regard. However I maintain the length of time has to be six days because of (a) the many parallels with the name covenant Jesus undertakes with Simon and the threshold of the Transfiguration; (b) the name and threshold covenants in the Creation week, separated by six days; (c) the name covenant Mary of Bethany undertook with Jesus and the Passover; (d) Yom Kippur and Sukkot (e) conception and implantation in the womb. All these issues are discussed at greater length in the previous books in this series: *God's Panoply*, *God's Pageantry* and especially *God's Pottery*.

6 Jacob's name is a picture of his birth. The Hebrew letter 'yod' (י), for hand, is

added to 'achov' (עקב) meaning *heel*, to create the name, יעקב, *the hand that grasps the heel*. (See: L. Grant Luton, *In His Own Words: Messianic Insights into the Hebrew Alphabet*, Beth Tikkun Publishing 1999) Since *heel* ('achov' or 'ackov') in Hebrew is also *if* ('eikev'), the primary word surrounding the action of *choice*, the sense of the name Jacob is also *the hand that lays hold of the choice*. In other words: *an opportunist, a manipulator, a deceiver*.

7   Perhaps Steven Collins is right: Abram was a mercenary warlord employed by Melchizedek and he wouldn't have got to keep the spoils anyway. (*Discovering the City of Sodom: The Fascinating, True Account of the Discovery of the Old Testament's Most Infamous City*, Steven Collins, Latayne C. Scott, Howard Books 2013) On the other hand, perhaps the word 'Melchizedek' was, as many suggest following Jewish tradition, a title rather than a name—for the man most revered in the world of the patriarchs: Shem, son of Noah. Still alive in the time of Abram and well over five hundred years of age, he would have seemed almost immortal, having out-lived many of his descendants. The eye-witness account of the flood could easily have been directly passed from Shem to Abram.

8   Quite probably not the same Abimelech. 'Abimelech' may well have been a title for the king of Gerar, as Pharaoh was a title for the ruler of Egypt.

9   Ezekiel 14:14. Of course, in a later age, Jesus would undoubtedly have made this list.

10 'In a sense, Job must replay the original test of the garden of Eden, with the bar raised higher. Living in paradise, Adam and Eve faced a best-case scenario for trusting God, who asked so little of them and showered down blessings. In a living hell, Job faces the worst case scenario: God asks so much, while curses rain down on him.' (*The Bible Jesus Read: Why the Old Testament Matters*, Philip Yancey, Zondervan 1999)

11 In this book you are holding, I assume you know what a threshold covenant is and what can go wrong with it. The basic text on what a threshold covenant is culturally and anthropologically-speaking is Henry Clay Trumball's *The Threshold Covenant*, which dates back to the nineteenth century. How it can go wrong and what issues result spiritually as a consequence of it going wrong are covered in two previous books in this series: *God's Pageantry* and *God's Pottery*.

12 Job 13:3, Job 31:35

13 Reflecting the words of the High Priest on the Day of Atonement. After placing his hands on the head of the scapegoat and confessing the sins of Israel, so that they would be laid on the goat, the High Priest would cleanse himself from top to toe. Putting on clean linen garments, he would approach the altar of sacrifice with its waiting bull and goat. Careful to avoid anything that might spoil the sacrifice, he would say to the attendant priests, 'Do not touch me, for I am not yet ascended.' (*The Messiah: His Comings!*, John O. Grimley, Xulon Press)

14 At least in that particular gospel.

15 As pointed out in *God's Poetry* and augmented in *God's Pageantry*, the first and third books in this series, this name has its origins in Talmai, the name of one of the giants of Hebron.

16 John 19:25—it should be noted that John reveals there are three Marys at the cross. It should also be noted that, if Mary, the wife of Cleopas was with him on the road to Emmaus, as early church tradition maintained, then Jesus favoured these three faithful Marys with an appearance on the day of His resurrection.

17 The early church writer, Hegesippus, claimed that Clopas was the brother of Joseph, the husband of Mary, Jesus' mother. That would make Mary and Cleopas the aunt and uncle of Jesus.

18 Cleopatra is often given as meaning *glory of the father*. However, it can also mean *keys of the father* or *keys of the fatherland*. Its male equivalent is Cleopas.

However, recognising that 'patra' may also be from the feminine form of 'petros', *rock*, it is possible, even probable, that the last element of Cleopatra's name is equivalent to Peter. Since Jesus was clearly using the name Peter in a multi-lingual pun, this suggests that the last part of the name may have more than one sense. It could be *rock* (as in *the start of an enterprise*), but it could also be *firstborn, the one who opens the way, the opening*.

Thus Cleopatra could also have resonances of *keys of the firstborn, keys for the start of an enterprise, keys of the opening*. That last seems a bit pedantic and redundant but it still makes sense. Also, the name may have overtones of *glory of the firstborn, glory for the start of an enterprise, glory of the opening*.

Of course, Cleopatra was killed by an asp. The word for *asp* in Hebrew is the same as for *python*. And it's related to the words, 'peor' and 'peter', *opening*. Cleopatra seems to have chosen a death in accord with her name.

But, this in turn suggests that the biblical name, Cleopas, is a threshold name. And that indeed seems to be the case since the incident at Emmaus is the undoing of threshold covenant defilement.

19 Matthew 16:18-20

20 Mythic: I like the fact that Rene Girard relates mythic to *mute*. It's not that 'mythic' is untrue but that it seeks to hide, sanitise and maintain a veiled silence about the violence of the true.

21 That is, the original 1984 version of the NIV. Check out the next footnote to see what's happened in the 21st century.

22 Oh, what an immense difference a few years can make to translation. There's no indication in the current NIV, apart from a note that the Hebrew is difficult to translate, that the former references to *mind* and *heart* have been substituted as follows: 'Who gives the *ibis* wisdom or gives the *rooster* understanding?' (Job 38:36 NIV) Here we seem to have a reference to Thoth—the ibis-headed god of the Egyptians—who was credited as the author of all works of science,

religion, philosophy, and magic. The Greeks were a little more specific that the Egyptians, declaring Thoth to be the inventor of astronomy, astrology, the science of numbers, mathematics, geometry, land surveying, medicine, botany, theology, civilized government, the alphabet, reading, writing, and oratory. They further claimed he was the true author of every work of every branch of knowledge, human and divine.

So, while 'ibis' is a good translator's choice for the mind as the 'seat of wisdom' symbolically and mythologically speaking, it doesn't seem to fit with Hebrew thought. Hence why I am choosing the former NIV translation over the latter.

23 If you've read *God's Panoply*, you will recognise this as another instance of a concept so alien to our western thinking that it's virtually untranslatable. We choose one or the other, never both. And we tend to be traditional in those translations. Throughout this series, I've looked at several such words that encode richly-doubled ideas: *kiss* and *armour*; *war* and *bread*; *sea* and *time*; *threshold* and *python*.

24 This looks to me like the origin of the Greek word, 'psyche'. The Greeks, however, saw *soul* as *butterfly*, not as *meteor*.

25 Had Elihu visited Abraham, prior to his visit to Job? Here he calls God 'Shaddai', a name only revealed to Abraham just a week or so before the destruction of Sodom.

26 *God's Pageantry* and *God's Panoply*.

27 A radiant vector refers to the point in the sky from which the meteor appears to originate. In this instance, the cosmic storm may have been the Orionids—the meteor shower that occurs in mid to late October as the earth passes through the orbit of stony fragments that were once part of Halley's Comet. Like the Māori description of Poutini, the Orionids originate in the constellation of Orion.

28 Truly this sounds like an exaggeration, doesn't it? 'Sea frozen like a stone'! *The Annals of the Four Masters* which records historical events in Ireland mentions a time when the Sea of Moyle between Scotland and Ireland was frozen over. This too sounds impossible but personally I believe it once happened: and that stories like Tolkien's legendarium of the crossing of the Grinding Ice by the elves of the Noldorin recall a deep race memory of that terrible event—a cold so intense that crossing the frozen sea in search of food was the only option. All that is needed for such a calamity is an impact winter, such as that which dendrochronologist Mike Baillie discovered has occurred in the sixth century.

And speaking of impact winter: why did Abraham immediately leave Hebron for Gerar after the threshold covenant with God? This, incidentally, was during the time when Lot had fled Sodom and was struggling through the suddenly uninhabited wilderness that eventually became Moab. I believe it's because the impact winter affected the grazing for Abraham's vast flocks and herds—he had to quickly move somewhere less influenced by the cosmic strike.

29   As I have mentioned in *God's Pageantry*, the answer to God's question, *'Where were you... when the morning stars sang for joy?'* is, because of the relativistic nature of the universe, 'Right here, right now.'

30   Owen and Hugh are actually related. They are said to come long ago from the same Celtic root, which a minority of books say is 'aed', *fire*, and the majority say is 'uis', *heart* or *soul*.

As I've remarked before, after a period of acquaintance with a name and its patterns, it's possible to get a feel for its song. So I was watching the movie *Smilla's Sense for Snow* when I realised that the symbolism was very 'hugh-ish'. It took only a moment to discover that the author of the original book *Miss Smilla's Feeling for Snow* was the Danish author, Peter Høeg. Was Høeg a form of Hugh?

There was no mention of the 'golden ratio' or 'golden mean' in the film but I decided it was the sort of thing that might get overlooked in Hollywood's obsessive pursuit of an action-packed plot. So I went out and bought two books by Høeg: *Miss Smilla's Feeling for Snow* and *Borderliners*. I started with *Borderliners* and I have to admit I was surprised at how far I got into the book before a mention of the 'golden mean' finally turned up—all of three pages! But there was no Owen. Indeed, the only character names that bore any similarity to each other in Høeg's two books were Issy and Hesse.

Although it didn't fit my pattern, once I'd become aware of Hess, it started to crop up as regularly as Owen or Hugh in relation to the golden ratio—continental writers tended towards it while English-speaking writers tended to use Owen.

More and more, I was puzzled. Why should any name be associated with any mathematical concept? And, even allowing that there was in this particular instance, why should there be an exclusive club of Owen, Hugh, Hess and their variants such as Owain, Eoghan, Gawain and Essen?

Years of investigation finally led me to a single remark by the German master philologist, Jakob Grimm, who is more famous for the folktales he collected with his brother Wilhelm. Grimm believed that it was likely that Teutonic Hess and Celtic Eoghan had the same root and they could be traced back to Gaul, possibly as long ago as the first century before Christ. He suggested the origin of both names was Esus.

I froze as I read those words. In case you haven't noticed this is perilously close to Jesus. Especially since the letter J was never used in the Greek classical world or the Hebrew Scriptures.

You've missed the entire significance of name covenants if you don't realise the implications: the likelihood that the names Jesus and Esus had got messily entangled with each other was extremely high.

Esus (also spelled Hesus) was a savage god, worshipped in forests with human sacrifices. The Germanic 'All-father' triple-god Odin probably has his origins in Esus. Zeus, the name of the lecherous Greek god who ruled Olympus, is also considered by some commentators to be another take on Esus.

Because of the very nature of names and their power, and also because our forefathers often hedged their bets when it came to worship, it is all too easy to subsume Esus into Jesus and unknowingly have a high place in our souls where we offer sacrifice to an unholy alliance of Jesus of Nazareth and another 'Jesus', be that 'Jesus' Zeus or Esus.

One of the reasons evangelism to Jews is so difficult is because they often equate the Greek name, Jesus, with Zeus.

31   One of which is Gaut, from which we derive the English word, 'god'. The translators of the Authorised Version of the Bible, commissioned by King James I, chose 'God' as a translation of Yahweh from amongst several possibilities. It's important to remember that the name does not actually belong to Odin: he just took it. All names belong to the Lord of all, the one from whom every family in heaven and on earth derives its name. (Ephesians 3:15)

32   Two of the top three of my favourite passages of Scripture turned out to be threshold-related. I sometimes wonder about the last one: 2 Timothy 2:11-13.

33   In my view, this is derived from 'sekviy'.

34   In Hebrew 'shaq' means *lintel*, and is related to *watchful* as well as having a resonance of to be *wakeful*. In Turkish, it has actually come down to us as *threshold*.

In *God's Pageantry*, the discussion of 'shaq' occurs in Chapter 2 in the section about the threshold covenant between God and Abraham. God gives Isaac—Yitshaq—a name that has 'threshold' overtones embedded within it. Many centuries later 'shaq' occurs in a punning interchange between God and Jeremiah which also has threshold undertones to it.

In *God's Poetry*, however, I point out that Isaac is a rhyme for 'esek', meaning *dispute* or *contention*—and this is an extremely apt for the shape of Isaac's life.

In *God's Pottery*, I point out that an understanding of the overtones of 'shaq' are necessary to be able to comprehend the suicidal game Abner proposed to Joab at the Pool of Gibeon in 2 Samuel 2.

35   Those who know the names of Hebrew letters will recognise this as the 'k' of the Jewish alphabet, meaning *the palm of the hand*. The palm of the hand has a shallow hollow in it and this is exactly the idea behind uses of 'kaph' as a word. For the Hebrews, it was not only a hand that had a palm, so did the foot. The palm of the foot (between the sole and the heel) also has a shallow hollow shape. The stone called 'kaph' has a hollow in it—not a deep hollow, just a shallow one to catch blood. The stone is placed at the doorway of a house, and,

because Middle Eastern doorways were at the corner of a house, they were the cornerstone. Thus a threshold stone is a cornerstone. (The reason I use term 'threshold stone', rather than 'cornerstone' is because too many people have preconceived ideas about cornerstones.) The uses of the many senses of the word 'kaph', particularly as detailed in chapters 18 and 19 of John's gospel, are detailed in *God's Pottery*.

36   There is no doubt an earlier one than this: between God and mankind in general. When Adam and Eve are driven from the Garden, there is an implied sacrifice which occurred at the gates of Eden. Here God seems to have demonstrated the shedding of blood for atonement and covenant.

37   Though spelt 'eb' in English in this particular instance.

38   Hebrew 'sullām'. At one point in my investigation of names, I wanted to find out what the fragment 'sul–' really meant. Sullivan and Suleiman (Solomon) were amongst the names I was looking at. I conjectured from my research that 'sul–' might mean *the falling sky* or *thing that falls out of the sky*. In an effort to look deeper into this, I delved into Toni Morrison's books, *Sula* and *Song of Solomon*. I felt that my conjectured meanings for 'sul–' were on the right track when I discovered the title character in *Sula* accidentally kills another character called Chicken Little. (Now, no one in the book ever squeals, 'The sky is falling! The sky is falling!' but is that really necessary with a name like Chicken Little?) Also in the book, when Sula returns to her hometown, all the birds fall out of the sky. As for *Song of Solomon*, I won't spoil the ending for you except to say that it fits the pattern of things falling out of the sky.

All this to lead up to the question: Is sullām a ladder? Or is it simply a thing that fell out of the sky?

39   The Hebrew is 'galam', folded together. The word 'golem' is derived from this; a 'golem' is a legendary animated clay being, shaped like a man, made by humans. Many 'gal' words are also related to stones.

'gal': *a heap* (generally *waves* but also *rock garden, rock pile, ruins, stone heaps*), derived from 'galal', *roll*

'gil': sometimes has the sense of rock: 'gilead', 'galeed' (*witness rock* on Mt Gilead)

Goliath, who was killed by a rock to the skull, 'gulgoleth', *skull* (though admittedly the text uses 'metsach').

Nonetheless, because 'gal' is often used in proximity to the use of stone, it is worth considering that 'galam' has the sense of *stone woven together*: thus human beings are woven stone.

40   I remember reading the whole of Philip Pullman's *His Dark Materials* trilogy, getting to the end, and thinking, 'Who on earth is Asriel? It seems like a compound name made up of the Norse word for *god*, the Celtic word for *king*

and the Hebrew word for *God* or *Lord*. Perhaps it means *lord and king of the gods*. But since Asriel clearly isn't the biblical God, which counterfeit is it?' I puzzled for several minutes before it dawned on me the answer should be on the first page—and, if not, then the first chapter. Actually when I went back, it turned out to be in the first line.

Now, it's not that I expect you to simply sit down, write a fairytale and expose all the right details. It takes some work of refinement. Write what you can, until you have a full-blown story—even if it's just the plot outline of the story—then work it over a little. Don't censor. Don't tidy up the theology. Treat your writing as a crucible of fire which is causing the dross to rise to the surface.

Keep a record of your dreams. Write down the strange words that pop into your head. Commit to paper—*paper*, not just a document file—all these, as well as any visions you may have. Trust in God that, one day, He'll send you the person who can translate these all for you.

41   See *God's Pottery*.

42   There are numerous other examples of name covenants—and even the possibility that the Hebrew word for threshold covenant was the origin of the word used to indicate tribal initiation. Bennelong had a friend whose name was anglicised as 'Colebee'. Midshipman Newton Fowell of the First Fleet flagship HMS Sirius called him 'Gringerry Kibba Coleby'. His first name, 'Gringerry' or 'Goungarree', meant *cuts in the chest*. And according to David Collins, his second name 'Kibba' came from *gibba*, *kibba* or *kebah*, which meant a *rock* or *stone* and was a term used to indicate that a man's front tooth had been knocked out by a stone during initiation. His third name, Colebee, came from his exchange with the Gweagal (Fire Clan) warrior Wárungin Wángubile Kólbi.

Cuts in the flesh of the wrist or palm were the oldest way of 'cutting covenant' and were the sign of a blood covenant. Later the Jewish people used the cut of circumcision instead as a sign of their covenant with God. Amongst the warriors of Australia who needed their hands for spear or boomerang-throwing and for whom scar tissue on the hands would make hunting more difficult, perhaps the transition to cuts in the chest is an obvious one.

Colebee's nephew, Nanbarry, exchanged names with Ballooderry, but gave up that name after Ballooderry's death.

See also Endnote 76 regarding 'gibba', 'kibba' and 'kebah'.

43   Matthew seems to indicate that this was the second test, not the third. However there's no real discrepancy in their accounts. Luke doesn't specify any particular order (Luke 4:9) and Matthew only indicates that the temptation on the high point of the Temple occurred after the temptation to turn stones into bread. (Matthew 4:5)

44   The Mount Zaphon of Canaanite myth was probably not originally Mount Hermon. But fluidity of geography is a feature of myth and legend the world

over. For more brief information on Typhon, see *God's Pageantry*.

45 For many other etymological reasons based on the various names of Mount Hermon why it should be identified as the Mount of Transfiguration, see *God's Panoply*.

46 Dwight Pryor in the article, *Jesus—The Fullness of Tanakh*, in the book, *Roots and Branches: Explorations in the Jewish Context of the Christian Faith*, discusses the Transfiguration at some length, pointing out that the language used by God during that momentous event is that of a midwife. He further points out that, just a few days prior to this, Jesus had asked His disciples who people thought He was and also who they thought He was. Several answers are given—but God's answer to Jesus' question is not revealed until the Transfiguration. His statement is a combination of phrases from the Law (Moses), the Prophets (Isaiah) and the sacred writings (Psalms). In addition, there are three witnesses to the Father's words, reflecting this same threefold division of Law, Prophets and sacred writings: Moses, Elijah and the Father Himself.

47 David Patterson, *Hebrew Language and Jewish Thought*, Routledge 2004

48 http://bit.ly/Vei4KD

49 This ancient sentinel who demanded the answer to a riddle is in many ways similar to the monstrous watchdog that guarded the gates to Hades, the Greek version of the Underworld. Cerberus, the offspring of Typhon (see Endnote 44) and Echidna, had a mane, along with the feet of a lion, the tail of a snake and three heads. These heads were sometimes depicted as belonging to dogs or sometimes, as in the Serapis cult, belonging to a lion, a dog and a wolf.

50 Or maybe they were the same pair who were sitting in the tomb when Mary Magdalene peered in. I never thought of it before the moment of writing this. Perhaps they accompanied Jesus for the whole forty days.

51 The last time 'miphtan' appears, it is in the curious statement: 'In the same day also will I punish all those that *leap over* the threshold [miphtan], which fill their masters' houses with violence and deceit.' Now, leaping over the threshold, or springing over it, is the essential meaning of 'Pesach', *Passover*. Everywhere else in Scripture, leaping over the threshold [kaph] is what God desires us to do. But here He promises to punish those to do so. The difference is that a miphtan is a threshold defiled by Python and therefore the action of leaping over such a threshold is one of coming into covenant with this spirit of constriction. God wants us to be covenantally one with Him, not with a cosmic being who squeezes, strangles, chokes and causes worry.

52 Isaiah 27:1 NIV

53 en.wikipedia.org/wiki/Lotan (accessed 25 September 16)

54 Isaiah 27:1 NIV

55 en.wikipedia.org/wiki/Lotan (accessed 25 September 16) Lotan is the 'mighty

one with seven heads'.

56   2 Peter 2:7-8 BSB says: '*Lot, a righteous man distressed by the depraved conduct of the lawless (for that righteous man, living among them day after day, was tormented in his righteous soul by the lawless deeds he saw and heard).*'

57   Another example of a turbulent threshold is the meeting of a river with the open sea. This 'threshold crossing' illustrates significant spiritual principles paralleled in the natural world. Sometimes a dangerous sandbar has to be negotiated safely. If you try to pass over on the wrong tide, at the wrong speed, on the wrong wave, with the wrong boat, your vessel can flip and your passengers injured or killed. This threshold to the open sea of 'destiny' requires all the conditions to be right, not just some of them.

58   In Ephesians 6:13, the Greek word, ἀναλάβετε—'anabalete', *take up*—is second person plural imperative. This means that it is a command to 'you all', not to the singular person. In addition, in Ephesians 6:11, the Greek word, ἐνδύσασθε—'endysasthe'—can not only mean *put on* or *clothe* but also *clothe another person*. There is astonishing resistance by some Christians to the idea that the armour is corporate, that is, for the whole of the local expression of the Body of Christ, and not for solely personal use. The failure to see that it is given to us so we can gird others with it through prayer is indicative of the rampant individualism and isolationism of this age. I've had someone 'unfriend' me on Facebook over my refusal to back down from my view that the armour is essentially for the community of believers and that we can pray for other believers to be clothed in it.

59   '"Delicacies" were so called because the food has been offered first to the idols of the... pagan gods. The pagan peoples of the ancient world ate the leftovers of foods sacrificed to their gods as a means of identifying with the gods.' (Michael Youssef, *Discover the Power of One: make your life count*.)

60   Just in case I was being too subtle there, I am referring to Darth Sidious who was the master of Darth Vader, the dark persona of Anakin Skywalker.

61   This symbolism may seem strange—that owls should symbolise vampires. However, the owl is the symbol of Lilith, the forerunner of all vampires.

62   Llyr appears to be the Celtic equivalent of the Roman god, Janus. According to the medieval historian, Geoffrey of Monmouth, Leir was once a king of Britain. The city of Leicester was named after him. His successor was a daughter, Queen Cordelia, who had him buried 'in a four-sided grave' on the banks of the River Soar. His tomb was in a chamber dedicated to Janus and craftsmen made pilgrimage to this site on the first day of the year. This ritual suggests that Leir was originally the god, Llyr, and that Janus was his Roman counterpart. Shakespeare adapted and built on the legend of Leir for his play, *King Lear*.

63   The half-comedy of the story was probably enhanced for the writer by this ironic detail: Ehud was a left-handed man belonging to a clan whose tribal

name means *son of the right hand*.

64   As far as Jewish rabbinical teaching is concerned, a falsehood that is spoken to save another person's life is not a sin. Most Christian commentators, however, consider there is no such thing as a 'righteous lie' despite what is said in James 2:25—'*...was not even Rahab the prostitute considered righteous for what she did when she gave lodging to the spies and sent them off in a different direction?*' (NIV) I find it curious that some of these commentators are nevertheless able to countenance the idea of 'righteous killing'.

65   Though what her specific crime is would be a matter for considerable debate, depending on our culture.

66   The Hebrew word for *lodging place*, 'malon', used in Exodus 4:24, seems to be a play on words—a combination of 'maal', *act treacherously*, and 'lun', *lodging*. Although it may not always be so in all usages of the word, certainly the first four occurrences of it in Scripture (out of a total of eight instances altogether) are to do with locations where acts of duplicity occurred.

67   He was also later called 'Jerub-besheth', meaning *shame will contend with him*. Joab uses this name as an example of a foolish military strategy when he sends a message to David that Uriah the Hittite has been killed in battle. This choice of example was no doubt Joab's not-so-subtle way of saying that David had much to be ashamed of, not just in arranging Uriah's death, but in the way it was accomplished—causing other unnecessary deaths.

68   Of course, it's quite possible, that although Judges 8:31 says it was Gideon who named Abimelech, it was at the instigation of his mother. She was a concubine (see Endnote 72) of Gideon from the town of Shechem.

69   http://www.dawntoduskpublications.com/html/oak_shechem_long.htm (accessed 3 September 2016)

70   You don't have to go far to find one. The NIV Study Bible has this in its footnotes.

71   In fact, based on the wordplay involving the name Gershom and the phrase, 'gar sam', meaning he *lived there*, Bethlehem may be the hometown of his father. Thus the town of Bethlehem is not only linked to the family of David, but also to the family of Moses.

72   A man's concubine was often not only a second wife but his cousin—married to keep the inheritance within the family. Steven Collins points out in *Discovering the City of Sodom: The Fascinating, True Account of the Discovery of the Old Testament's Most Infamous City* (Steven Collins, Latayne C. Scott, Howard Books 2013) that Keturah may have been a cousin of Abraham. It's possible therefore that Jonathan's concubine may also have been his cousin.

73   Here's another threshold allusion within the story: Jerusalem/Jebus is just within the territory of Benjamin—on the border.

74   1 Samuel 11:7 NIV describes the actions of Saul as, in this very same place

many years later, he cuts up some bullocks as a call to war: *'He took a pair of oxen, cut them into pieces, and sent the pieces by messengers throughout Israel, proclaiming, "This is what will be done to the oxen of anyone who does not follow Saul and Samuel." Then the terror of the Lord fell on the people, and they came out together as one.'*

75   Samuel's father comes from the hill country of Ephraim, as indicated in the very first verse of the first book of Samuel. The significance of Saul's friendship with Samuel should not be pushed to the background: it is sufficient reason for deep suspicion by the people of Bethlehem who see the alliance as a source of potential trouble. When Samuel turns up one day looking to anoint one of Jesse's sons, they wonder if he's come in peace; or whether some pretext for war is about to be revealed.

76   Both 'bora' rings and 'bora' trees are significant in the culture of the Australian First Nation peoples. (Trees associated with ceremonial sites or boundary markers are called *teleteglyphs* and trees associated with burial sites are known as *taphoglyphs*.)

The majority of bora rings were to be found in northern NSW and into south-east Queensland—at least 120 stone circles or mounds have been documented in that corner alone. The word 'bora' is said to be derived from a Kamilaroi word, 'bor' or 'boor', *the belt of manhood*. However, the *belt* may derive its name from the *ring*, rather than the *ring* from the *belt*. The word 'bora' has also long been employed to denote the ceremony of initiation that took place at bora rings.

Other indigenous words were employed for the 'bora ring' by different tribal groups:

'Jeraeil' used by the Kurnai.

'Kuringal' used by the Ngarego.

'Bunon' used by the Yuin and the Murring of the coast for a ring with a mound. 'Kadja-wallung' used by the same tribes for a ring without a mound.

'Yoolahng' used by the Fire Clan, the Gweagal of Port Jackson, the tribe which practised name exchange as mentioned in Endnote 42.

'Burbung' used by the Wonghi or Wonghibon and the Wiradjuri. The Wiradjuri also used the name 'Guringal', similar to the 'Kuringal' of the Ngarego.

'Cawarra' used by the clans around the Macleay and Nambucca Rivers.

'Kabbarah' is the term used by the Port Macquarie tribes.

'Kipparah' used by the clans around the Wilson and Hastings Rivers.

'Bora' is the name used by both the Kamilaroi of the New England plateau of Northern NSW and the Cheepara tribe from the region south of Brisbane.

(https://downloads.newcastle.edu.au/library/cultural%20collections/pdf/etheridge3.pdf)

The word 'bora' seems obviously related to the ending of 'kabbarah' with its clear linguistic affinity to 'kipparah', to 'cawarra' and to 'burbung'. In addition, other linguistic associations can be seen in words linked with initiation ceremonies such as 'kippa', 'gibba', 'kibba' or 'kebah'. 'Kippa' allegedly means *young man* or *manhood* in the dialects around Brisbane and Redcliffe and is now used to describe bora rings in that area. The words 'gibba', 'kibba' or 'kebah', according to David Collins, meant a *rock* or *stone* and was a term used to indicate that a man's front tooth had been knocked out by a stone during initiation.

In my view there is a strong possibility that these words are all ultimately derived from the interrelated Hebrew word set—kaph, kaphowr, kippur, kapporeth, kaphar—which are to do with *thresholds, stones*, and the *cutting of covenant.*

For at least some clans, bora rings were associated with boundaries and thresholds. Colleen Wall said: *'When people came into my country they would wait at bora rings which were located at entry points into country.'* (http://bit.ly/2gSrdon)

The crossing over of young boys to manhood using a ring of stones echoes the crossing over of the children of Israel into maturity in the land of promise. After the crossing of the Jordan, the Israelites came to Gilgal and covenanted at an altar of twelve stones. Like Gilgal, indigenous word markers for 'bora' include Kuringal and Guringal, both of which end with the Hebrew word for a *stone heap*.

The age at which young boys pass over into manhood is around the same as Jewish boys experience their 'bar mitzvah'—*son of the commandment*—ceremony. The bar mitzvah ceremony ratifies the covenant of circumcision that occurred when they were eight days old. Many indigenous Australian bora ceremonies included circumcision, reflecting the Arabic tradition of circumcising boys at thirteen—the same age at which Abraham's son, Ishmael, was circumcised. Within a few days of that circumcision, God cut a threshold covenant with Abraham.

Sufficient words and ceremonial actions bear such close relationship to each other across Hebrew and numerous indigenous dialects it is possible these bora ring rites go back to a memory of that primeval covenant between God and man. If that is so, then the destruction of bora rings by incoming peoples from outside Australia is a covenant violation, bringing with it attendant curses for such desecration. Albert Dennison makes a remarkable statement about bora rings in Kamilaroi country: *'The Serpentine is another important area for us, but not as important as Boobera. ... There are important sites all over this country. There are bora grounds on the cotton fields out there. You can see them from the air, because nothing will grow there.'*

(austlii.edu.au/au/journals/IndigLawB/2001/9.html)

That statement, *'nothing will grow there'*, recalls the Scriptural consequences of threshold covenant violation: a barren landscape or famine.

77   This comment is found on page 75 in *The Emmaus Mystery—Discovering Evidence for the Risen Christ*, Continuum Books, 2005. I think Thiede must have been referring to German translators in this instance because this parallelism is not reflected in the English versions I have consulted. (I have occasionally noted the issue highlighted here: I can spend years researching a particular topic, painstakingly piecing together tiny pieces of the jigsaw—only to find the theory I have put together so slowly and with such enormous difficulty is common knowledge or a widely-held assumption in a European academic culture where my language skills are deficient.

78   I was reading a really good book recently which, for its own sake, remains nameless—because it stated categorically Moses had failed to circumcise his sons because of his wife's opposition. When she relented, God stopped opposing him. This seemed to me to be an extensive extrapolation of the text and, if not a bit misogynistic, then at least a haloed view of Moses as the unblemished hero.

79   Each of these covenantal seals has some significant connection with the number seven. The rainbow of course has seven colours. The rite of circumcision is traditionally nowadays performed seven days after the day of birth. The Sabbath is the rest of the seventh day. The temple built at the direction of Solomon was constructed over a period of seven years by the seventh son of David. David in some genealogies is given as a seventh son and in others as an eighth. His wife, Bathsheba, Solomon's mother had a name meaning *daughter of the sevenfold oath*. And, in yet another seven, the temple was built on one of seven hills of Jerusalem. The seal of the new covenant of grace and peace is the Holy Spirit who is sevenfold in nature.

80   Sapphira, probably meaning sapphire or lapis lazuli, from *caphar*. A play on the word for threshold (mentioned in Acts 5:9) or else, by allusion, for judgment.

81   See *God's Pottery* for details.

82   See *God's Pottery* for a discussion.

83   The principles which follow in this section are an adaptation of the primary laws which make life unmanageable as expounded by many healing prayer ministries. The purpose of healing prayer is sanctification to equip and empower individuals to be transformed and then pass their healing on to others, so the process of discipleship can be truly walked out in daily life.

84   Job 41:15-16

85   The symbol of the healing snake uplifted on a staff has an obvious counterfeit in the entwined serpents of Asclepius, the son of Apollo in Greek legend. He was the god of healing whose symbols were the snake and the cock. The famous last words of Socrates, as reported by Plato, were: 'I owe a cock to Asclepius.' Modern medical symbolism is derived from the staff or rod of Asclepius.

86   Arthur Burk in *Joy Unstoppable* makes the important observation that many modern translations, such as the NIV, prefer *creatures* to *people*. However he also points out that the Hebrew word, 'am', which appears here also comes up over a thousand more times in Scripture and, in *every other* instance, it is translated *people*.

87   Abarim Publications, abarim-publications.com/Meaning/Pethor (accessed 16 November 2016)

88   1 Chronicles 9:20

89   See *God's Pottery*.

90   He also seems to have been given a name covenant, though it's not made explicit. However his name in the text briefly acquires an extra 'yod', normally understood as *the hand of God*.

91   http://www.yashanet.com/studies/revstudy/rev2h.htm (accessed 6 December 2016)

92   *Four Prophets: Amos, Hosea, Micah, Isaiah 1–35*, JB Phillips, Geoffrey Bles 1963

93   Yechiel Eckstein, Holy Land Moments Daily Devotional, *May Your Will Be Done*, 12 June 2015

94   Al Houghton, *Jesus & Justice*, Word at Work Ministries.

95   Note that Joshua seems to have learned his lesson from the mistakes of Moses. Once the people had crossed the threshold of the Jordan—and it is clearly meant to be understood as a spiritual threshold since the term used for the crossing is 'pass over'—he immediately ordered the men to be circumcised at Gilgal. This is precisely what Moses should have done when God called him back to Egypt. He should not have waited for Zipporah to do it. Joshua passed a test at this point. Although he was to make mistakes in the future, they were very different to the ones Moses made.

96   John Day, *God's Conflict with the Dragon and the Sea: Echoes of a Canaanite Myth in the Old Testament*, CUP Archive 1985.

97   Or 72, the number given in Luke 10:1. In either case, the number seems to refer back to the elders of the tribes who ascended Mount Sinai at God's invitation to have a banquet with Him. Exodus 24:9 refers to seventy elders plus Nadab and Abihu, who later died when they offered unauthorised fire before the Lord. Later in Numbers 11:25, the Spirit of the Lord rests on seventy elders at the tent, plus Eldad and Medad who were outside in the camp. Clearly, therefore, the number seventy is symbolically equivalent to the number seventy-two when either is being used in connection with a representative council of the servants of the Lord and His people.

98   The word 'mot' may be deliberately used at this point rather than 'palats' in order to better allude to Zaphon, death and divine judgment. In the Baal-Anat cycle of Ugaritic mythology, the Canaanite god of death and the underworld,

Mot, attacked the king of the gods, Baal, in his palace on Mount Zaphon, precipitating a war between the gods. This allusion ties the psalm so neatly to Mount Hermon (as 'Zaphon') that it confirms, yet again, for me that it is the site of the Transfiguration. Furthermore, one significant reason Jesus ascended the mountain was to fulfil the prophecy of the psalm: He stood up in the assembly of the gods and challenged them. The words of divine approval given by His Father were not simply the words of a midwife, guarding the name-seed of church as it matured in a spiritual womb, they were also a decree passing judgment on the gods of the nations who had not acted justly and who were now doomed to die. 'Mot' with its overtones of the underworld, death, the foreign Canaanite pantheon, judgment and the shaking of nations works perfectly in this context. Just before going up the mountain, Jesus in a brilliant contemporary alignment spoke of the 'gates of Hades', referring in a single concise phrase to the underworld, death, a foreign Greek pantheon, judgment and the shaking of nations.

99   Peles, *weigh*, is to do metaphorically with *judgment*. Perhaps the *trembling of a scale pan* as it weighs is the common thread that runs from *shudder* (palats) to *weigh* (peles) to *judge* (palal) to *entreat* (palal) to *deliver* (palat).

100 Those two verses make the subtle distinction between the results of confessing to God and confessing to each other: in the first instance, we are forgiven; in the second, we are healed.

101 Nor is it like the verbal sacrilege that could be epitomised by the words of yacht skipper Dennis Conner just after the fourth race in the America's Cup in 1983. For 132 years, no contender had successfully challenged the perennial victors, the United States. At the end of the fourth race, Conner said seven words that, in my view, changed that.

Before 1983, nationalistic pride in Australia was almost miniscule. Australians like to say we won the Cup; but, in my view, the Americans simply lost.

What did Dennis Conner say? You won't find it in any official record, but it's etched deep in my memory. I happened to catch the television broadcast just after *Liberty* had won the fourth race. Conner knew another win for his yacht would clinch the Cup—whereas the Australians would have to win three straight.

'We cannot lose,' he told an interviewer. 'God is an American.'

132 years of history were on Conner's side but I knew instantly it wasn't enough. 'God doesn't often defend His name,' I thought. 'But I think He's about to. *Australia II* is about to do the impossible.'

Yes, what Conner said was blasphemy. Mostly, however, it was unmitigated stupidity. God probably made a distinction between the two—but the outcome was the same. Sometimes we need to remember that.

www.ingramcontent.com/pod-product-compliance
Lightning Source LLC
Chambersburg PA
CBHW021104080526
44587CB00010B/368